In this hurried life, we can become s
unmoved by God's glory all around
to there, missing the beauty of his works. In *All Shall Be Well*, Catherine McNiel slows us down and takes us on a journey of seeing and believing. God is found in the beauty and the pain, the flowers and the thistles. His goodness to us is enjoyed by pondering his wonders.

KYLE IDLEMAN, bestselling author of *Not a Fan* and *Don't Give Up*

This book has done more than *teach* me: It has *nourished me*. *All Shall Be Well*, rich in imagery, theological depth, and soulful introspection, is exactly the kind of book I like to read and recommend. McNiel grapples insightfully with the paradoxes of being human and loving this beautiful, broken world. I want more and more people to read her valuable work.

JEN POLLOCK MICHEL, author of *Surprised by Paradox*

All Shall Be Well beautifully and poetically reveals the seasons of life. From the dead of winter to the promise of spring, Catherine McNiel teaches us that our God is present and listening, calling and leading no matter what our circumstances are. She reminds us that our faith is a journey of spiritual formation, a character-shaping relationship with the Creator God. Nature calls; read this book.

CALEB KALTENBACH, author of *Messy Grace* and *God of Tomorrow*

With her trademark insight and beautiful writing style, Catherine McNiel leads readers like she's our personal spiritual director. She invites us to wonder at God's mysterious presence, while continually pointing her readers to God's renewal of all things—to the spring in our winters. If you're longing to connect deeply with God and with his messy, abundant creation, you will find those longings expressed—and met—in these pages.

AUBREY SAMPSON, author of *The Louder Song* and *Overcomer*

"Our God is not far off. From the very beginning, Christians have declared that the Creator is not only *transcendent* but *immanent*." With these words, Catherine McNiel plants the foundation for an ingrained display of God's beauty and goodness among us. While we often wonder where he is amidst the thorns and weeds, *All Shall Be Well* reminds us that God is still here, tending his garden . . . for us.

ALAN NOBLE, award-winning author of *Disruptive Witness*

If you enjoy Barbara Brown Taylor, you'll love Catherine McNiel. She awakens us to the cathedral of the everyday, the altar that calls us to worship.

TRICIA LOTT WILLIFORD, author of *You Can Do This* and *Just. You. Wait.*

I want to write like Catherine McNiel when I grow up! With rich insight and delicious turn of phrase, this book gently replants the reader's soul in the seasons. This is a truly helpful work for those of us who don't know what to do with our anxiety, restlessness, and creative yearnings. McNiel gives us the ground from which to say, "All shall be well," regardless of the season of soul in which we currently reside.

CASEY TYGRETT, author of *As I Recall* and *Becoming Curious*; host of the *otherWISE* podcast

Grounding, lyrical, and rich with meditation and metaphors, McNiel turns our eyes to the wonders of God all around us and invites us to cultivate simple practices of awareness.

ED CYZEWSKI, author of *Flee, Be Silent, Pray*

With vibrant and poetic words that touch all the senses, Catherine invites us into an intimate connection with our creator, no matter the season in which we find ourselves—even the dark days of winter. Then, not wanting to leave us without practical tips, she provides simple yet profound disciplines to cultivate life in the Kingdom now. This is a book I'll return to again and again.

KELLYE FABIAN, author of *Sacred Questions*

I am the weary traveler McNiel is writing to, and her book is such a tender invitation to trust, to rest, and to embrace whatever season I find myself in. Through prose saturated with kindness and clarity, she provides a much-needed reminder that the life I'm seeking is not found in the busyness, or the chaos, or the things that overwhelm me, but in the beauty of nature and the goodness of God. The "Cultivating" sections at the end of each chapter provide practical steps that feel less like a to-do list and more like mile-markers on a path to the divine.

SHAWN SMUCKER, author of *Once We Were Strangers* and *Light from Distant Stars*

Catherine McNiel's prose is, itself, further evidence of the abounding beauty of a world touched by God's presence. *All Shall Be Well* will open your eyes to the lush and lively wonder of his redemption in every season and every situation.

JASON HAGUE, author of *Aching Joy*

Catherine's writing is more than beautiful. It is transcendent. Seen through her eyes, the everydayness of living bursts forth with abundance, spiritual meaning, and God himself. Catherine is a wise soul, and her readers will enjoy this journey with her through the spiritual seasons of life. I greatly appreciate and highly recommend this book.

VALERIE BELL, CEO of Awana

ALL SHALL BE WELL

ALL SHALL BE WELL

Awakening to God's Presence in His Messy, Abundant World

CATHERINE MCNIEL

NavPress®

A NavPress resource published in alliance with Tyndale House Publishers, Inc.

NavPress®

NavPress is the publishing ministry of The Navigators, an international Christian organization and leader in personal spiritual development. NavPress is committed to helping people grow spiritually and enjoy lives of meaning and hope through personal and group resources that are biblically rooted, culturally relevant, and highly practical.

For more information, visit www.NavPress.com.

All Shall Be Well: Awakening to God's Presence in His Messy, Abundant World

A NavPress resource published in alliance with Tyndale House Publishers, Inc.

The Team: Don Pape, Publisher; Caitlyn Carlson, Acquisitions Editor; Elizabeth Schroll, Copy Editor; Eva M. Winters, Designer

Published in association with the literary agent Don Gates of The Gates Group, www.the-gates-group.com.

For information about special discounts for bulk purchases, please contact Tyndale House Publishers at csresponse@tyndale.com, or call 1-800-323-9400.

Cataloging-in-Publication Data is available.

ISBN 978-1-63146-977-0

Printed in the United States of America

25 24 23 22 21 20 19
7 6 5 4 3 2 1

For my Dad:
Thank you for teaching me to garden,
and for letting me sit on your lap and read
theology over your shoulder.
I've always been proud that you were my pastor.

And for Matthew:
I met you in the final days of spring,
and we've walked side by side all this long, hard summer.
Take my hand as we enter the close of autumn,
and, finally, the snows of winter.
There is no one I would rather travel with than you.

Instructions for living a life:
Pay attention.
Be astonished.
Tell about it.

MARY OLIVER

To live is so startling it leaves little time for anything else.

EMILY DICKINSON

CONTENTS

FOREWORD

CATHERINE MCNIEL'S *All Shall Be Well* is a fresh, visionary work about an ongoing life of faith that breathes and grows in us organically—a garden of beauty and contrast that allows the senses to fully and joyfully play, echoing the fervor of a Creator who displays a profound satisfaction with the universe he has spoken into being. God saw the beauty he had performed in the creation as it came to be, concluding with this remarkable statement on the final day: "This is more than 'good.' It is 'very good,'" an expression that might well be expressed as divine enthusism: "This is truly glorious!"

All. Shall. Be. Well. Four simple yet profound syllables form a comprehensive, declarative statement spoken with such emphasis and conviction that it captures our attention. Readers often value these words recorded among the sayings of Julian of Norwich, the fourteenth-century cloistered visionary who heard such reassurance from God in direct but mystical "showings" that her certainty has comforted generations of troubled and doubting souls ever since. In anxious times, when fear takes over, we are heartened to believe that all shall indeed be well under the loving, overarching hand of our God. This is an act of faith. This is what trust looks like.

Catherine brings this theme to life by echoing the words of some of our most celebrated poets and writers—Mary Oliver, Emily Dickinson, the church fathers, and other theologians and philosophers—whose words gain new life and light as they reflect each other's wisdom. She has suffused her soul with the rude stuff of creation—the soil and the stars. Beauty but also bane, a viridian green but also the faded brown of decayed organic matter that ends up being humus, a fertile cultivar for new growth. Vivid color, along with brilliant light and startling contrast, brings this theme into our reach in fresh and vital ways. Our souls respond. Our lives expand with this new challenge.

Catherine also offers a soul-warming dose of *shalom*, that word that encompasses the idea of wholeness, health, peace. And then she shatters the mirror and presents the contrasting chill of doubt and unknowing, where our faith is in a God beyond and above us, a God we cannot fully understand, but who proves himself to us, even in trial, by supplying divine strength and sustenance that carry us again into a place of blessing and safety—where again All. Shall. Be. Well.

Luci Shaw
Bellingham, Washington

OPENING

THE GARDEN

Here is the world. Beautiful and terrible things will happen. Don't be afraid.

FREDERICK BUECHNER, *WISHFUL THINKING*

Then the LORD God planted a garden . . .

GENESIS 2:8, NLT

WHEN THE CURTAIN rises for the very first time, the Gardener is alone on the stage. He's wearing dungarees, as they used to call them; overalls. He's kneeling in the dirt, digging hands into the soil. Planting a garden.

He's muddy, of course. Gardening is full-body, hands-on work, and the Gardener is covered in soil past his elbows and knees. When he stands up to stretch, his muddy arm smears earth across his brow.

Taking a moment to survey his accomplishments, he nods with delight—*yes, this is good*—then kneels and continues planting. He works carefully, lovingly, intentionally. He hums and whistles unself-consciously, for this is his joy, his creation. This is on purpose. This is good. This is *his*.

With a final pat of the ground, the garden is in.

And now, something else.

Turning away from his burgeoning garden, he approaches a fresh piece of earth. Lifting clay out of the ground, he molds it, forms it. Again—lovingly, carefully, joyfully—he fashions the dirt into the shape of his design, his own image. He stands back to admire the work.

Yes, this is good. This is *very* good.

Then something incredible happens.

The Gardener lifts the finished work in his arms and leans down, placing his face on its face, his eyes to its eyes, his mouth to its mouth—and breathes. He breathes his own sacred, holy, living breath into the image he fashioned from the dust.

And it becomes a living thing.

Seek and Find

Friend, this is our origin story, our family tree.[1] *We* are what the Gardener formed so long ago—you and me and folks ten thousand miles away, the mountains and oceans and prairies, the mosquitoes buzzing around my porch light, the dandelions growing through the cracks in your sidewalk. His garden covers the earth; his breath fills the universe. It has become you and me and all living things.

Psalm 19 says that creation proclaims the truth about the Creator—day after day, night after night.[2] Without speech or sound or words, this voice carries to the end of the world, and in this noiseless declaration, God teaches us, right here among the earth and sky, trees and flowers, neighbors, children, and creepy-crawlies. The Gardener entreats us to step into the world he made and walk with him, to receive from his hand the daily bread our bodies, minds, and hearts so deeply crave. We are the clay that God is still molding, still nurturing, through the repetition of cycles and seasons, in the mess and abundance of our daily lives.

But there is a problem, a foil: We modern humans rarely look for truth in the soil and stars. In fact, we scarcely spend time outside. I live in a factory-made world of concrete and central heating, buying processed food and clothes with little idea how to trace these shrink-wrapped items back to their origins in the ground. Since we think of truth as residing in words and ideas, we tend to limit seeking God to such things, seldom even noticing the cycles of living and dying that govern our lives—or receiving the wisdom he offers through them.

I wonder about the spiritual atrophy[3] we experience by living cut off from the earth. In how many countless ways have we lost the ability to seek and find our Creator? We've worked so hard to isolate ourselves from the realities of creatureliness, but have we also removed ourselves from God's provision, the wisdom and sustenance he offers? We desperately thirst for something more but have grown unseeing, unhearing, unable to absorb the truth and glory always proclaimed by earth and sky.

People sometimes describe themselves as "spiritual but not religious," but in my circles we often show symptoms of the opposite aliment: We memorize verses and learn facts, and we're prepared to defend them; our doctrinal statements are read and signed. Sometimes it seems we'd rather categorize God than *be with him*. We opt for merely signing off on God's résumé.

But faith is a journey of spiritual formation, a character-shaping relationship with the living God. Robert K. Johnston describes our dilemma perfectly:

> In the vestibule of an auditorium there were two doors. Above the one door was a sign labeled "heaven." Above the other door was a sign labeled "lecture about heaven." And people flocked through the door labeled "lecture."[4]

Even back in the Garden, Adam and Eve fell into trouble when they adopted the habit of talking *about* God rather than speaking *to* him. Suddenly, the Gardener began to appear not quite as life-giving and intimate, perhaps not entirely trustworthy. From there, the relationship was all-too-easily broken.

We do this still, losing intimacy and trust when we avoid talking *to* someone and instead talk *about* them. How much more so with the one who made us and knows us inside out? Time and again, we slide into this pattern, speculating and debating about God rather than searching for him.

But he is here.

Our God is not far off. From the very beginning, Christians have declared that the Creator is not only *transcendent* but *immanent.* In his transcendence, God is perfect, whole, other. This means we cannot grasp or tame him, we cannot overpower or domesticate him. Yet God is also immanent: crucially, palpably present. Wherever we go, all we must do is lift our faces, hold out our hands, or take in a breath—and find him here with us.

Can you imagine the trouble we'd be in if God were only one of these? If God was near but not sovereign, our hope would be frail, like second-brew tea or weak coffee. If he were transcendent but not present—well, isn't that the actual definition of hell?

He has promised to meet us, he has promised to be found—if we can open our distracted, weary, frightened eyes and *see.*

Flower and Thorn

But there's good reason for our hesitancy; we know all too well that where there are flowers, there are thorns. There's suffering here, and death. Injustice and pain churn around us, blinding and disorienting us like swirling snow. That's the thing about this garden, and we must acknowledge it straight away: There is beauty so brilliant and penetrating it can break your heart—but there is every bit as much struggle, pain, despair, and death. We get bogged down, overwhelmed, encompassed by the unrelenting darkness. How could a world so full of trouble and pain warrant careful attention, be worth lingering in?

Yet I'm convinced that God can be found in both: the beauty and the pain.

Today it's cold with freezing rain where I live—December 21, the winter solstice. We've been weaving our way toward darkness and chill since late June, the pinnacle of light and warmth. Even at noon, with the curtains thrown back, there isn't enough natural light to read or work by. Dim lightbulbs attempt to compensate, but the coziness they lend to winter evenings is simply depressing in midday. The chill in the air reminds me of last chances, last stands, out of time, out of hope.

Yet these are my favorite hours of the year. The winter solstice is a sacred day, when hope imperceptibly strikes the fatal blow to despair. On the darkest day, during the longest night, we turn the corner. Something happens that cannot be perceived: The light is coming, and though we see or feel nothing at all, what *will be* is certain and cannot be undone. Like so many victories, it is silent, "already-not-yet."

To me, the solstice is a message for weary travelers, a sign embedded into creation pointing the way to the truth—again and again, year after year. There's a reason Christians celebrate the coming of God as a baby during the week of solstice. Holding Christmas candles in the dark, we declare: "The true light that gives light to everyone [is] coming into the world."[5] And while the cycling seasons could never convey the incredible story that *God was born* and pitched his tent among us, the good news I read in the Bible comes alive in my mind and heart while watching the light break into darkness each December. I need this annual lesson to sink deeply into my spirit and take root there, for the garden we live in is not just flowers and sun.

Years ago, during a season peppered with confusion and despair, I somehow heard God coaxing me, calling me to come outside and meet him. And so I did, walking into a grassy field littered with wildflowers. Closing my eyes, I heard him asking me to rejoice, to take off my shoes, to run and dance with joy.

But I refused. No, I couldn't, I wouldn't. Instead, I sat down, paralyzed. I showed him—or rather, he showed me—my heart: that I was so afraid. I knew from years of experience that hidden among the beautiful flowers and grasses were sharp thorns, angry wasps, blunt rocks. If I threw restraint to the wind and rejoiced here, in this meadow, I would find myself crippled with pain, falling, bleeding.

Surely, I countered, you cannot ask me to do *that.* Surely, this rejoicing-with-abandon is for the naive, for those who have not yet been scarred by the reality hidden beneath the beauty.

But his voice was gentle and firm—he *did* ask this of me. To stand and worship without restraint, fully and entirely aware that this life holds both beauty and pain, joy and suffering. *Because he is here.*

In light and dark, in life and death, in joy and sorrow, *he is present, and we can find him.* We can listen for that still, small voice in the rustling of leaves or the crashing of waves, not idolizing creation but delighting in the Creator. Waking up to his presence in the beauty of early morning or the chaos of life is *worship*, the joyful practice the Gardener invited us to live by when he fashioned this world by hand. We humans have always learned best through repetition, and God's lessons replay themselves for us day after day, year after year.

So now, in these pages, I extend this invitation to you: Will you wake up, step outside, look around yourself, and ask, *Where am I today? Where is God in the midst of it all, and what creative, redemptive work is he doing here? What is he teaching me, how is he feeding and forming me, in this season?*

With our hearts firmly rooted in his words and our feet firmly planted on the ground, let us walk courageously into this garden, this messy, abundant world—with all its beauty and all its thorns—and find the nourishment we crave. At the end of each chapter, I suggest a few practices you might bring along as you step out of these words and back into your own life; a few tasks that may help these ideas imprint on you. If you find one that is rewarding, I encourage you to return to it as a regular practice.

His hand is outstretched, coaxing you today, friend. Knowing what you know—of the flowers and the thorns, of life and death, of joy and pain—will you open your eyes, stand up, and accept his invitation? In everything God made, there is something we need that will point us to him. In every season, there is something we need to learn. Will you awaken and receive the provision he placed upon this earth?

He is right here, waiting.

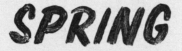

SPRING

1.

the earliest, usually the most attractive, period of the existence of something[1]

2.

to grow as a plant

3.

to issue by birth or descent

4.

to come into being: arise[2]

CHAPTER 1

THAWING

Hope

Hope is a path on the mountainside. At first there is no path. But then there are people passing that way. And there is a path.

LU XUN, CHINESE ESSAYIST, 1921

Hope is being able to see that there is light despite all of the darkness.

DESMOND TUTU, IN AN INTERVIEW WITH *THE NEW YORK TIMES*

WINTER HOLDS ON tight, this early-March morning; I'm beginning to despair that it will ever end. But today is Ash Wednesday, the first day of Lent. My family and I crowd the church aisle, jostling each other a bit as we stand in line. We came here to mark a sign of early spring: the cross of ash etched on our foreheads.

This season of spiritual preparation reflects our current reality precisely. *Lenten* means "springtime" in Middle English, which itself comes from the word *lengthen*.[1] The sun arches back toward us, leaning in to life, sunlight hours growing longer each day. The darkness has not won; the world *will* thaw again. It is time to prepare for new life. The ashes on my head are the charred remains of last year's Palm Sunday branches, declaring that we have gone around the cycle once more: Life retreated to death, now doubling back toward life.

But not yet.

Hope comes bundled with endurance and long waits in ambiguity. We have been barren and cold, but life was not entirely snuffed out. We endured and held on for the thaw to come. Hope builds the bridge that pulls us out of suffering and points us toward the path—the arduous, winding, uphill climb—leading, eventually, to joy. Hope steps out boldly and brings an umbrella.

Leaving the church, we encounter the most amazing surprise: a breath of warm, fresh air. Sunshine. Mountains of snow dissolve everywhere, shrinking, dripping, soaking, forming trickles running headlong into babbling brooks along my street curb. Bundled in my coat and boots, I drink in every drop of this miracle. Have we made it? Did we survive the darkness and cold? Is it time to come alive again?

Then I see it, the sign I have been waiting for: a sliver of green, peeking through the crystals of melting snow. The first shoot of the first spring flower.

In the early morning light of this new day, fresh air fills my lungs, defrosting my winterized body as newly formed rivulets dancing over the ground fill my ears. Plenty of ebbs and flows lie ahead as the days lengthen toward warmth and light; plenty more ice and cold will come before springtime wins out.

But today, there is something new. Our dripping, melting, now-muddy yard turns my thoughts toward life and fullness. The ashes on my forehead remind me, long before Resurrection Day, to begin, to prepare the way. What was alive is now dead—from the brown, withered leaves in my yard to last year's celebration palms, now ashes on my skin. We step outside to gather the decaying flora not because of grief but because of hope.

Life is coming.

Shalom

Since time began, the earth has spun its inhabitants through a yearlong drama of life and death and life again. The springtime chapter of this drama hints at the ultimate redemption: *shalom*. This ancient Hebrew word means *wholeness*, and it describes a world where everything is put right.[2] Not just one or two things settled and lovely but all creation in harmony. One author describes it like this:

> The webbing together of God, humans, and all creation in justice, fulfillment, and delight is what the Hebrew prophets call *shalom*. We call it peace, but it means far more than mere peace of mind or a cease-fire between enemies. In the Bible, shalom means *universal flourishing, wholeness, and delight*—a rich state of affairs in which natural needs are satisfied and natural gifts fruitfully employed, a state of affairs that inspires joyful wonder as its Creator and Savior opens doors and welcomes the creatures in whom he delights. Shalom, in other words, is the way things ought to be.[3]

This is what the Gardener was singing about as he nurtured each tiny seedling in his garden, as he breathed life into all living things. Shalom has been our destination all along, the shape God has in mind as he molds and forms us.

But our world clearly doesn't overflow with wholeness just now. From our most intimate relationships to the most global affairs—and everything in between—we are at war. Conflict and catastrophe pervade every community, group, and interaction between you and me, us and them, people and nature, children and parents, future and past.

Yet we believe the days are lengthening. From the garden beginning to the eternal city of light at the end, the Christian account of the world is a story of hope. We are a people of eschatology, citizens of a Kingdom that has been promised and begun, but not yet seen. We journey through darkness, bearing crushing burdens and devastating realties, but we have heard the notes of a beautiful song. As Jürgen Moltmann says: "From first to last, and not merely in the epilogue, Christianity is eschatology, is hope . . . the glow that suffuses everything here in the dawn of an expected new day."[4]

But do not mistake hope for *safety*. Hope breaks us open. Hope is never naive to suffering, is synonymous not with optimism but with courage. Hope knows with certainty that life overflows with both beauty and pain, and we cannot know which will rise to meet us. Trembling with possibility, hope sidles up boldly to despair, nestles close, and puts down roots. These two—hope and despair—stand always side by side, each determined to outlast the other. If we choose hope, we must join the standoff, with hearts and hands wide open, fighting the urge to fade into despair.

Not all that comes to life in spring will survive. All the most precious things are vulnerable; one new life will die quickly, suddenly, while another thrives and grows. Others will lie dormant, blossoming only after hope has faded. Life offers no guarantees. Except, perhaps, this one: We will, all of us, encounter beauty and pain, both so gripping and vast they will rock us to the core. These are the terms, the facts of life. And in full realization, we open our eyes and hearts to another year of what-may-be. There is no alternate way forward.

It's so much easier for us to keep our hearts closed and hardened, isn't it? When our eyes open to the pain, the danger, the trouble, it takes courage to pry our hearts open long enough to come alive. But when we live closed off and hardened, we pave over the garden with concrete; we shut the door to possibility, to coming alive.

The apostle Paul was well acquainted with this ever-present tension between hope and despair. He exhorts his readers to hang on to hope, to find our courage in the undying love of God even as the world offers no protection against death. As he says, "In this hope we were saved. But hope that is seen is no hope at all. Who hopes for what they already have?"[5]

Then,

> If God is for us, who can be against us? . . . Who shall separate us from the love of Christ? Shall trouble or hardship or persecution or famine or nakedness or danger or sword? . . . No, in all these things we are more than conquerors through him who loved us. For I am convinced that neither death nor life, neither angels nor demons, neither the present nor the future, nor any powers, neither height nor depth, nor anything else in all creation, will be able to separate us from the love of God that is in Christ Jesus our Lord.[6]

Yes, darkness looms, palpable. The groaning is real, and despair always whispers at our backs. But the Christian faith centers itself, from first to last, in the hope of shalom, that redemption will come not only for you and me but *for all creation*. That the guarantor of this promise is none other than the Creator himself. That "creation itself will be liberated from its bondage to decay and brought into the freedom and glory of the children of God."[7]

And so, we begin. In spring, we declare that light and shalom are gaining ground. That ultimately, the Creator will breathe new life into the dead bones piled all around us. Fully aware of the fine print on life's binding contract, we carry on, one step in front of the next, pouring ourselves into the void, into the future. Into hope.

On the heels of winter, born out of the broken shell of death, new life bursts forth. We are so vulnerable, so fragile; the risk is high, the chances uncertain. Surely floods and drought, weeds and pests will assail us. Openhearted, we tenaciously offer everything we are to the same world notorious for its fierce tendency to utterly destroy.

We believe that in the end, every bit of creation shall be caught up and made new.

The Facts of Life

When you live in the north, as I do, *thawing* can take your breath away. We have made it through months of bitterly cold dark days and nights. We speak of "surviving" winter without exaggeration: even now, the shelter, food, heat, and immune system required to endure these months cannot be taken for granted; not everyone makes it through. Death comes in winter. We see it all around.

But then, almost imperceptibly, springtime invites us to come alive. Green grass reaches up from black soil, birds sit determinedly on nests, the first brave daffodils burst forth, and if you look closely enough, you can see tiny buds on the trees. Kids strip down to T-shirts and shorts and start running—I've been known to join them myself. It's as though our own tenacious desire to *live again* flings open the season, as though in our spirits, we're all cooped-up children along with the birds and buds. We will find redemption here if it kills us. We scramble to get out of the house and let our spirits soar in the almost-warmth like a newly born colt stretching long legs for the first time. Nature faithfully continues the gorgeous, spellbinding drama of life and death it has cycled through for unfathomable ages—and we humans are every bit included.

As the northern ground comes alive from months of frozen death, my family and I dig up the soil. We plant tiny, microscopic seeds and tentative, fragile seedlings. Buried in the elements, they begin to open, to take root, to come alive. Soil is the mother of all life.

But soil itself is death.

The rich black layers of compost that we spread over the garden each spring are the grass cuttings, table scraps, and rotten tomatoes of last year. Collected over months, foul and decayed, this life-giving substance embodies life turned to death—ready now to receive and give, ready to become the womb of new life.

On this Earth, there are no exceptions. We were formed from the dust, and to dust we will return—as Ecclesiastes reminds us.[8] We are fashioned and every day sustained from life that has died and only through death was transformed to become the womb of another living being. Eventually we, too, will be put in the ground to nourish and nurture new life.

I'll be the first to admit: It is hard to accept these terms. When it comes to life, I am greedy, insatiable. I want the life side of the coin without the death side. I want to dance without paying the piper. I know I'm not alone in this. We push against the reality of death, hardly believing that our allotted turn will come swiftly and surely to an end, that everyone we love is like the grass of the fields.[9]

And yet, death *itself* is not the enemy.

From my vantage point—where my loved ones and I form the center of the universe—death certainly appears dressed to kill, the limiting factor in my greed for life. But when I step outside my own desires, I see something much bigger and more beautiful at play, a drama of creation and redemption as unfathomably vast and long-standing as the universe. A dance set in motion by God himself.

Death and life, together as one, form the great paradox. They introduce themselves as opposites yet come to us always intermingled. Neither can exist alone. Within this paradox, we live out every day given us. The irony is that, if we could in our greed destroy death, we would not open the doors to everlasting life, but rather to the *cessation* of life. One cannot exist without the other.

And yet . . .

Christians believe that two thousand years ago, the Creator entered this world as *part of creation*. He was born and lived as any human does. And then, in Jesus, God walked all the way up to death and surrendered, allowing himself to be consumed.

Consumed, but not contained.

The boundaries could not confine him, the center could not hold. Death began to explode, unravel, become undone. By dying, our Creator destroyed the reality of death.

Jesus became the firstfruits of hope, of a new harvest, a harbinger of a new world—one that is not born and fed from decay. A life that does *not* end in death. An eternal thaw.

N. T. Wright says, "This is part of the point of Easter that is very hard for us to think about: Easter commands us to think about a non-corruptible physicality, about a physical world that isn't subject to decay and death anymore."[10]

I read Wright's words on Easter Day to my eleven-year-old son, and he pondered them. "A garden that can grow forever, without compost? Without soil?" he asked, incredulously.

Yes. This is the incredible, astonishing hope of the Resurrection: a life without death. A garden without soil.

Can it be? This sort of earth is literally impossible, unbelievable.

And yet, as a Christian, I choose to step into this hope, into this lengthening toward shalom. I choose to believe that the Creator *can and will* release an encore that retains the beauty without the pain. I choose to stand inside the Kingdom of God and the hope of resurrection. A world where strength exists without injustice, where delight exists without poverty, where love exists without hate, and where life exists without death.

We use this word *hope* so poorly. We say, "I hope we get pizza for dinner," but this is desire, a counterfeit. *Hope* fortifies desire with trust, with faith, with desperateness and risk. Hope grows deeply rooted, with much to lose and much to gain, unafraid to look loss, disappointment, and despair in the face while still proclaiming its courageous message: The most powerful forces in the universe may yet be those of life and love.

And so, we begin. The Gardener is at work, and we are a people of eschatology, doggedly joining our Creator, kneeling in the dirt and the rubble, sorting through the broken things with an eye for redemption. We are looking for him everywhere, dusting for his fingerprints. We are building a world brand-new on the debris of the world destroyed . . . again, and again, and again.

With our arms covered in compost, gently packing seeds into the womb of death, my family and I step into the perilous wonder of spring: the hope of a world made new.

CULTIVATING HOPE

No matter how dark and cold your life may be today, new life is beginning somewhere. Remember that hope begins before we perceive it, lying almost dormant in a season of near death. Where do you see signs of thawing? Where is hope starting to break through? What is coming to life in your home, family, community? In your heart, your mind, your spirit?

- **Walk outside and take inventory.** Whatever the season or weather in your portion of the earth, allow yourself a moment to take it in, to soak up the newness and miracle of future hope. Take a deep breath, then another. Remind yourself to *notice* this work of God in creation when you step outside, rather than just hurrying past.
- **Look inside and reflect.** God is at work, right now. What new life is God calling forth in you?
- **Develop a habit of recording signs of life.** When you peer into the darkness of your life and find a sliver of God's light, leave

reminders for yourself (perhaps a calendar notification or a note on the mirror). Collect these and look back on them when times get hard, and remember hope dawning in the darkness, God's shalom breaking through.

CHAPTER 2

CLOUDS

Faith

Now faith is the substance of things hoped
for, the evidence of things not seen.

HEBREWS 11:1, KJV

For man does not see God by his own powers;
but when He pleases He is seen . . . by whom
He wills, and when He wills, and as He wills.

THE WRITINGS OF IRENAEUS, VOL. I

I GREW UP in the country, and for years, my home was miles away from town. From our windows, we could see forests and prairies, wheat fields and cornstalks, dirt roads and tractors. If we ventured too far off the path, swarms of living things rose up to greet us, undeterred and unwilling to be swatted away. Sometimes deer or the occasional bear wandered, curiously, right up to the house.

But at times, we could see nothing at all. On a moonless night, the darkness was complete. And during the cool, damp months of spring, dense fog settled over our low-lying lake country.

I loved driving home on the winding country roads that

curved around lakes and marshes. But late at night, in the dark, surrounded by fog (and years before cell phones!), this could be a frightening journey. I recall one slow night drive in particular, feeling my way along a dirt road I could not see, trying to avoid the muddy ditch. I crept along, poking my head out the window for a better view.

Being unable to grasp where you are, or find the road ahead, can be terrifying.

Had I been walking along this familiar road on a spring evening, the mist obscuring my sight would have been exhilarating, as much-loved landmarks floated in and out of sight, shrouded in swirling cloud, every moment lovely, breathtaking. An enticing, enchanting evening. But the dangers of navigating a car at thirty miles per hour drained away all the magic and whimsy.

The trouble with cloudy pathways is that we don't want to wait. We want to plunge ahead, drive through, get to the end. We want to understand and grasp and move on. But control is an illusion more fleeting than the spring mist rising along the lake, a phantom vanishing in a moment.

We don't like to hang suspended; we prefer to arrive. But if we can summon the courage to linger and look, mystery may captivate us—and offer exactly what we need.

Cloud and Fire

The Hebrew wanderers wake each morning, not at home as each one of them imagines in the seconds before consciousness, but on the ground, again. In the wilderness. Panic threatens, never lagging far behind. Staring down terror becomes a daily tradition. *Where are we? Will we die with our children in this endless wasteland?* Their former life, as terrible as it was, at least offered predictability, certainty. *Remember the warm fires back home? Remember the warm meals? Yes, but remember the slavery, the oppression, the death. Remember that first and foremost.*

So, sure. Salvation is wonderful. Liberation is what they hardly dared dream of. But for what? To what end?

What good is it to die here in the wilderness?

Each day, they weigh this argument—some out loud, others behind locked faces. *Does this journey lead toward salvation, or merely out of the pot and into the flames?*

Lying on the hard ground in the moments before dawn, they stare upward, where a fire hovers above them in the sky, blazing with light and warmth. Soon it will fade into a cloud, a cooling mist against the punishing heat of the desert sun. But it remains always, immovable, hovering before them, leading the way.

It appeared first as they ran for their lives, away from Egypt, away from their captors. It didn't seem possible they would escape but then . . . this cloud. Guiding them. Obscuring their enemies.

When it stops, they stop and go about the work of daily living underneath its strange presence, pitching camp directly beneath. This cloud is Yahweh, always, always evident in their midst. They are never ever alone.

Is this a comfort? Sometimes. The one who called them out remains visible—a wonder so great you wouldn't imagine there could be room left for doubt or fear. But doubt and fear remain in good measure, for this constant presence means constant surrender, perpetually giving up control. This state of unknowing calls for such courageous faith. They can do nothing but follow when the cloud moves forward, nothing but stop and wait when it rests. They have no *choice* at all, no information to discuss, no long-term plan to weigh and perfect over time. Only waiting, trusting, obeying.

Or—more likely—complaining, grumbling, worrying.

Only this mist always before them. Only this mystery that demands surrender.

Today, so many thousands of years and miles away, I love this story, this image. I love that during the Israelites' flight from suffering to salvation (which led not through lush countrysides flowing with milk and honey but through the wilderness, the place of chaos and death), God was *present.* They could *see him.* He persisted always before them, active and visible. He appeared to them as a cloud.

These ancient people received no overarching strategy. God did not point the way forward with a GPS map calling out where to go next. He did not offer glimpses of the big picture or step-by-step instructions outlining their progression from "here" to "there."

No, God gave his children the hard task of following him into the wilderness, then offered them the gift of his presence. They saw only the next step . . . and then the next. They didn't know *where* they were going, where this cloud would lead or when. But they knew he was there. Right in front, leading the way.

The moment of God *actually, physically appearing* is called a *theophany*: God's physical presence to comfort and guide, to give life in the desert and light in the darkness.[1] God's Spirit coming near to dwell like a neighbor, like a bird settling into a nest, was called *Shekinah*, the veiled-yet-tangible dwelling of divine presence.[2] Can you imagine a greater gift? In the cloud and fire, God's presence lingered throughout the entire journey, visible every second of the day and night. He was present not only to Moses, or the prophets, or the saints, but to the entire nation of terrified pilgrims leaving Egypt for a future they hoped would not end in the barren wilderness.

We're in the same boat today, more or less. We follow God through a haze, blown away by glimpses of his presence but longing for more than a glimpse, for something solid. The life of faith demands surrender, for none of us knows what's coming. We can never see where the future will take us, only that he's here before us. This mystery both enchants and terrifies. If we could, we'd wrestle God into a formula, something we could own and argue and control. And yet, something powerful comes to life deep within us when we stop wrestling and rest in his presence—and remain there, abiding day in and day out.

It didn't take the Hebrews long to tire of living in mystery. Maybe they didn't tire, exactly. Maybe none of us can stay on a straight line for long when we can't see where we're going. So when Moses, their leader, left them behind to speak directly with Yahweh—was *enveloped* by the cloud for forty days and forty nights—well, I can see how they lost their way. That's a long time to be left alone in the wilderness. I can imagine how their confidence crumbled, how doubt turned to anxiety and blossomed into panic, because it happens to me all the time. My faith goes stale like wilderness manna, and I'm desperate for something—anything—solid, tangible, knowable. Sometimes even bad news goes down easier than unknowing.

By the time Moses came back, the people had taken matters into their own hands and built an idol, a calf they could see and touch. This seemed so much more comforting than trailing after a cloud.

We love to ridicule these ancient folks for their faithlessness, but honestly, I don't have a stone to throw. I doubt I would have found the faith to follow a cloud into the wilderness in the first place.

Christians don't worship statues, but we do love to center our faith upon certainty, forming something predictable we can arrange in proper order and hold tightly. "A lot of what we call faith is actually idolatry," suggests author Debbie Blue.[3] Like the Israelites, we're dying to leave the mystery behind for an idol, to form God, life, and the future into something that makes sense, something certain—set in stone. Something we can name and own and say, "I understand this, and so I am at peace." But God, and this life he made, are *living* and complicated. Sometimes we just can't handle the wildness of it all. As Blue says,

> There's a weird thing about the Christian faith: faith. It's thoroughly dependent on the existence of an Other who is profoundly alive and always a little outside the sphere of what we know, dependent on something that is not in our control, something definitely beyond our grasp, beyond grasping. Faith is more about depending on things unseen, things incomprehensible, than it is about making things sacred or ordering our world.[4]

So count me among the Israelites throwing gold jewelry at Aaron to fashion me an idol. A statue may be dead and loveless, but it is solid and certain and can be controlled, even mastered. An idol won't ask me to follow blindly when it moves into the desert and then to rest contentedly when it comes to a stop, no questions asked or answered.

But a statue cannot tenderly provide, will not rejoice over you with singing—so there's a trade-off here. A living God can love and be loved, can know and be known—but not controlled. A living God must be worshiped, surrendered to. So we must choose: Which life do we want?

The truth is that we are shrouded, every one of us bewildered, concealed, tangled, encompassed. No peeking ahead into the future, only the next step—and faith in his presence. We so easily become disoriented and obfuscated. Everything—everything—depends on whether we can trust the one who is with us, before us.

As it happens, the wilderness was not the only time God appeared to the Israelites as a cloud. Decades later, the wilderness wandering was over, a nation established, a king on the throne, and a temple built. Now, at last, the sacred Ark of the Covenant, which symbolized Yahweh's presence and contained the stone tablets Moses had received within the cloud, was brought to its proper home in the inner sanctum of the Temple, the Holy of Holies.

But at this moment, as the priests, musicians, and instruments raised their voices in praise, the Temple filled with a cloud; the glory of God's presence billowed so thick, the holy men could not even continue the ceremony.[5]

How exactly like our immanent-yet-transcendent God to show up so entirely that all our ceremonies must grind to a halt and surrender to his mysterious-yet-consuming presence. Each of our sacred rituals, ideas, and places draw us near to him, but not one can contain him. He destroys every idol with himself.

Unknowing

Approaching a mystery can be dangerous, though; terrifying. We rarely understand—and if we think we do, we're likely more turned around than we thought. It is all too easy to go off course. We may, a thousand times, take a wrong turn or get twisted around. But God, in his inscrutability, does not play tricks. He is here. He is calling us with near-infinite patience. Like the shepherd searching the wilderness for the one wandering lamb, he won't let us stumble away too far. If we open our eyes and our hearts and seek, we will find.

Not entirely. Not perfectly. Perhaps not immediately. But glimpses, over time. He does reward those who earnestly seek him.[6] Living within mystery is not a prison sentence but an invitation to flourish.

So how do we approach this wild, living love of God? We're following a good and faithful Creator who reveals himself as a cloud and does not offer formulas. We know of his nature through Jesus, through the Scriptures, through tradition and our own experience and stories—but we can never fully know the ineffable. He transcends every idea we generate, shatters every box we build to contain him. And yet we long to meet him, to rest in his presence, to taste and see him ourselves and be comforted. This is a longing that he created, and the voice calling to us is his own. He draws us to himself.

In an ancient book called *The Cloud of Unknowing*, an anonymous writer from fourteenth-century England showed us how to enter into this mystery:

> This is what you are to do: lift your heart up to the Lord, with a gentle stirring of love desiring him for his own sake and not for his gifts. Center all your attention and desire on him and let this be the sole concern of your mind and heart. . . .
>
> And so diligently persevere until you feel joy in it. For in the beginning it is usual to feel nothing but a kind of darkness about your mind, or as it were, a *cloud of unknowing*. . . . But learn to be at home in this darkness. Return to it as often as you can, letting your spirit cry out to him whom you love. For if, in this life, you hope to feel and see God as he is in himself it must be within this darkness and this cloud.[7]

Unfortunately, entering a cloud to find God is not currently in vogue. Post-Enlightenment Christianity fixates on two aspects of religion: knowledge and piety.[8] As disciples of this faith, we are trained to hold tightly to certainty and right behavior. But to what end? While knowledge and piety encompass two deeply important aspects of faith, they are not the whole package. Our predicament reminds me of the endless lecture on heaven, when heaven itself awaits—for our God is alive; and not only that, he is *present*, inviting us into a dynamic life of relationship. I am not content in knowing my children are alive, providing them food and clothing as needed: I long for us to know each other, to be together in the unpredictable blessing of relationship.

Can we find the faith to sit in the mystery of unknowing and be enveloped by his loving presence?

Spring Cleaning

My preschoolers shadowed me as I did a bit of spring cleaning, spraying and wiping down the large windows in our home. As I worked, they peppered me with questions, as always. *Could God lift a house? Is God stronger than a giant crane? Is God bigger than the whole world? If God is everywhere, does that mean he* is *the whole world?*

These are typical childhood "God questions," but they're not easy to answer. It's all part of the mystery we work so hard to form into stone. Yes, God could lift a house—except, he's not material, he's Spirit. And yes, God is stronger than a crane—but he doesn't have muscles. My children's image of the Creator must be something like the mythical Atlas, holding the world up with his biceps. Yet my own conception of God, though more socially acceptable and informed by decades of study, is probably just as pale in comparison to the real thing.

And so, as we scrubbed the dirt off our windows to allow the spring sun to shine in, I told my little ones that there are things we know for sure about God—he created us and loves us, he has a plan and we can trust him. He is holy and merciful and just and wants us to follow him. But our imaginations just can't grasp what he's really like. In fact . . .

I looked down at the damp window-washing rags in my hand and realized what a perfect time it was for this conversation.

The apostle Paul wrote that it's like we're looking at God through a dark, dirty glass. We can make something out, but we can't see the details. It's enough to show us he's there, but not enough to put a face to it. Faith is, after all, "the substance of things hoped for, the evidence of things not seen."

Then Paul goes on to say that someday, we'll see God face-to-face. We'll know him fully, just as he has always known us. Someday, faith will become sight.

My children and I peered through the half-cleaned, half-dirty window glass we were washing together. "Wow," they said.

Wow indeed. The dirt and chaos in my house is a small metaphor for the injustice, suffering, and chaos that fill this life we live. My babies are just starting this journey, just beginning to encounter the depth of the mystery and struggle we each must learn to face. The courage to step into an unknown world with the living God must be born into their spirits, for neither my children nor I have imaginations capable of picturing a Being strong and good and *everything* enough to bring a groaning creation to full redemption.

But we can see through the glass, dimly.

In the spring, we can see maybe just a bit more.

CULTIVATING FAITH

As much as we love to plan the future, truthfully, none of us can see the path ahead, at all. Life will come as it comes. Like the people of Israel following a cloud into the wilderness, we can see God before us but rarely have any true sense of where he is taking us.

Where are you walking through clouds today? Perhaps the present and future are confusing. Perhaps in this season, even God's character or the path toward him feels unknowable, unsteady. Perhaps these days are as full of disillusionment and painful confusion as they are with new life. Or perhaps you are finally free from the stone idols you have clung to, joyfully stepping into the adventure of the unknown.

Whatever the mystery, God is here too.

- **Make a list** of the unknowable things that haunt or excite you today. What are you planning, creating, hoping for?

- **Lift each of these things to the Lord,** confessing a tendency to grasp, an inability to control, an anxiety about trusting.
- Make time to simply **sit in the mystery.** Don't try to talk over the silence. Just sit before him, accepting this moment for what it is.
- Take care not to form these things into stone, into idols. Ask for help **stepping forth in faith,** trusting God but allowing the wildness of life to be what it is and will be.

CHAPTER 3

BEAUTY

Intimacy

When all is said and done, spring is the main reason for Wow. Spring is crazy, being all hope and beauty and glory. She is the resurrection.

ANNE LAMOTT, *HELP, THANKS, WOW*

Surely the LORD is in this place, and I was not aware of it. . . . This is none other than the house of God; this is the gate of heaven.

JACOB, SON OF ABRAHAM, GENESIS 28:16-17

TODAY IS WARM sunshine on my hair, cool garden soil between my fingers. The world is full of flowers, and I mean *full* of flowers. Dogwoods, redbuds, and magnolias line every street. I count over seventy tulips in my yard, and over half of them now form bouquets inside my house. And behold the gigantic lilac bush right outside the kitchen door, a sort of purple descendant of the burning bush. This fellow desperately needs a trim, but every autumn I don't notice, and every spring I can't bring myself to cut back the loveliness. The lavender cloud hovers so heavily it bombards innocent passersby, and the heady fragrance of all this sensual music occasionally sends me fleeing for fresh air.

Life brims over now, the days getting longer and the sun rising higher. Sunshine pours into my kitchen in the mornings, as we sit happily half-blinded at the table, munching our cereal and breathing in flowers. Sunshine lights up the living room in the afternoons, while in the evenings, dusty beams still play peekaboo through the shades as I put my children to bed.

It's easier to hear the music of life in the springtime. All creation is jubilant, redolent, and God throws flower-petal confetti everywhere. I can see the song, and I can smell the song, so there must *be* a song.[1]

In the midst of so much beauty, joy gives trouble a run for its money. Despair is wiped down as redemption bombards us, cleansing and making all things new. God's presence awaits us, inviting, dancing, his love embodied and made tangible all around. The Creator plays impishly, calling us to awaken and join him, running up and tagging us with laughter and crab-apple blossoms.

Intimacy with the Creator is a basic need, like food and air and family. My soul *longs* for God, the psalmist sings, *thirsts* for him, like a dry and weary land with no water.[2] These ancient words still ring true to our experience three thousand years later. That God actually inhabits this earth, living here among us—well, that is not a trivial matter. We so deeply need his love to be real, to be near. Have you ever felt discontent, restless, on edge—then been interrupted by a sunset, a smile, a song? He meets us, somehow, startling us out of our routine. Even a taste can keep us going. Even one day in his house is better than a thousand elsewhere.[3]

But why are we so parched? I have such grand plans to seek him in my daily breath and bread, in the snatches of silence and the chaos of his good gifts—but then, somehow, I don't. I don't remember to peer just beneath the surface and find my Creator's love upholding each moment of each day. He is here, always, everywhere, yet we forget to seek, have such difficulty finding. Like frustrated, tantruming toddlers, too exhausted to know what will truly bring comfort, we wear ourselves out rather than rest in his steady arms. We forget he is hiding in plain sight.

"Seek me and find me," he invites. "Come to me and rest."[4] But from the moment I wake until I lay my troubled heart and spinning mind on the pillow, there are emails to write and crises to avert, so many tasks and troubles. He can be found in all these things—but I forget to lift my face to his. I keep my head down while the moments and days bleed together into decades.

Mercifully, he doesn't let us wander lost forever. He's left reminders, interruptions, all over this world he made. Like the family photos we hang around our living rooms and offices, glimpses of him surround us. Encounters with beauty shake me awake despite myself. God's nearness becomes easier to touch, like low-hanging fruit, branches weighed down by heavy blossoms, tangling up in my hair as I rush by. God drifts with the pollen on the breeze, falling from the sky like petals, pushing through the earth like an onslaught of lilies.

Each one of them proclaims the glory of his presence. As the poet-theologian Rich Mullins sang, "Everywhere I go, I see you."[5]

I'm grateful that God always runs down the road to meet his prodigal sons and daughters, even when we're still a long way off. Too often we imagine him standoffish, demanding that we plead and cajole him to come near. But no, our salvation is that he is here already, watching for *us*, inviting *us* to come near.

I'd like to get better at meeting him halfway.

For me, finding God often happens by accident, when beauty startles me out of distraction. But there are ways to wake up at more regular intervals.

The ancient Prayer of Examen, instituted and practiced by St. Ignatius of Loyola, aims to help us "develop a reflective habit of mind that is constantly attuned to God's presence,"[6] to become detectives of God's love amid daily life. Ignatius considered this awareness so important that he asked his followers to complete this exercise twice a day—midday and evening—even if life allowed no time for other spiritual practices.

Like a recipe, the steps can be followed to the letter or adjusted a bit to meet your specific needs, but the basic flow is this:

- Remind yourself of God's presence. Step into his light and love, ask for eyes to see, remind yourself that he is here.

- Look around yourself with gratitude. Give thanks for the details of *this day* and *this moment*.
- Consider the feelings, emotions, and thoughts this day has stirred. Invite God into them.
- Reflect on what is wrong, broken, or painful. Ask for forgiveness, or the strength to forgive, heal, restore.
- Look forward to the coming moments or days. Ask God to walk with you and for a reminder of his presence.

Each of these five steps awakens us to God's presence *here*, the intimacy we can step into *now*. By God's grace, he's already running down the road toward us. Immanuel, God is with us. He waits only for us to behold.

This interruption of spring loveliness strikes me as the perfect time to begin.

Sacramental Beholding

On this sunny afternoon, I drive through the forest with a rare moment alone and thirty minutes to spare. Inertia fights hard, telling me to stay in the car, run some errands, start on dinner, keep driving.

Instead, I stop.

Leaving my car, I flee into the trees, then slow myself down and spin quietly around. There's so much to take in here. I could walk, gawking at the towering hills and trees, or I could be still, absorbing my surroundings slowly, immersed in a million details, the countless facets of life unspooling on this very spot.

Someone once said that any object can teach us if we take the time to look and really see it. One theologian suggested that "anything that awakens, enlivens, and expands the imagination, opens the vision, and enriches the sensitivity of any human being is a religious act."[7] He called this way of seeing "sacramental beholding"—which strikes me as the perfect picture of this intimacy habit I'm trying to cultivate.

Wandering through the forest, I move through the five steps:

God, you are here. Will you open my eyes?

Thank you for this place, and a moment to rest, to breathe. I see the trees, the water; I feel the fresh air pouring into my lungs.

Lord, I feel so rushed and busy, and it is hard to stop, to focus on you. Yet you are here in every chaotic moment.

I am weighed down with so many burdens, the pain from the past month blinds me. But I pour it all out at your feet. Will you help me carry these burdens?

Walk with me now down this path. I know you will but . . . help me remember.

It's easy to awaken here. This is his palace, the house of God, and I see signs of him everywhere. The sprigs of new, green grass peeking through the brown; the countless naked twigs pointing toward the sun, yearning for buds to appear; even the airplane high above, leaving behind a double trail of white in its wake, a zipper in the sky. All of it enchants me when I take the time to see it. Everywhere

I look, something draws me in and envelops me. My eyes open, and I behold.

I'm almost tempted to take off my shoes on this holy, sacred ground. Such a powerful teacher, this looking and listening. God is here, his presence announced loudly without words, offering the intimacy with him that we desperately need.

It surrounds us every day, but do we *look*? Will we allow ourselves to be met, and known, and loved?

I've meandered to the lake and stand at the water's edge, my toes curling around the far end of the dock. I've wiggled myself as close as possible without getting wet, surrounded by quietly rippling water, by hills smothered in trees. Circling it all, the vast expanse of blue sky solidly, unflappably pronounces infinity. The water comes alive with leaping fish and over a hundred ducks who have come here to play and mate and eat and *be*—living their lives abundantly in the presence of God, as they were created to do.

I see *him* reflected in this rippling lake he invented. I feel his warmth on my face as the sun touches my cheeks. I breathe it all in, mind, heart, and spirit opening to the living world all around me—as *I* was created to do.

It is too early in the year to linger here and enjoy it, really. I'm too chilly, and I hate being cold. Yet I can't pull myself away. Wrapped in a sweater, I stay on and on. Something here encircles me, and I let it take me; I am immersed, sinking, consumed. Truth speaks to me in a song, a poem, instructing me in a place far deeper than words. This is unadulterated creation, and everything—every droplet of water, every bit of air and soil, and all the life that lives within them—proclaims his presence *right here and now*.

How can I pull myself away from this magnificent tabernacle?

This earth and all its creatures, including me—we were made for each other. God intended this when he planted his garden, and we lose something beautiful and true when we live our lives removed. Even more so, we lose strands of intimacy and fellowship with the Author of it all. Where better to find him than on this earth he made, where he came to rest and walked among us?

Art Unveils the Artist

One of my best friends is an artist,[8] and while I personally can hardly use a crayon, even I appreciate the beauty in her paintings. Watching an idea swirl around her heart and mind, then around her palette and canvas, I see *her* come through in every stroke. The finished pieces clearly reflect the truth and meaning inside her soul.

This is what art does—it reveals the artist. If someone you loved deeply—your partner, parent, sibling, child—was a painter investing everything into her masterpieces, can you imagine having no interest in seeing the finished piece? As her work became known and beloved all around the world, as thousands admired and studied the pieces, attempting to discover the artist's mind behind them, can you imagine having no interest at all? You, who love this artist so deeply, have never seen a single piece.

This is impossible, isn't it? When our beloved ones create, we are their number one fans and supporters, the first to see a masterpiece-in-progress, to offer constructive feedback. The first in line on opening night, standing proudly by their side.

And yet, the one we love—who calls *us* Beloved—created and is creating the entire world and it proclaims him day and night. He is present here, relishing every piece. He invites us to join him, to walk with him.

We often consider nature apart from ourselves, *other.* A destination, a tourist attraction. We go out to see nature like we go to the store or to the movies. Yet we *are* nature. We were formed from dust, and to dust each of us returns. Every rock and puddle and bug and plant forms part of the same system into which we were born and live and into which we will one day die, adding our own cells to the ground to create more creation.

What is he teaching us as we cycle in and out of days, year after year, generation after generation? Will we listen and hear it? Can we walk outside and receive these truths, allowing beauty to reach our minds through fingers and lips, eyes and nose? Will we let *life* seep in?

Today, the sun's energy shines upon the earth, and a billon plants receive and convert this warmth into life and nutrition. Later, we eat these plants ourselves, or an animal does, which we then consume months later. In a wondrous miracle of creation, the energy that builds and sustains my body's cells is the same strength pouring from the sky, awakening the flora and fauna.

This cycle was once the most familiar thing of all, observed and understood by everyone. But today, hidden away from "nature," how much do we know of the cycles of life—of which we are part and which are part of us, which we alter and which alter us? How at home do we feel in these ever-repeating circles of life and death? Do we let them awaken our senses, open our vision, and offer a moment of sacramental beholding? How shall we learn to enter his redemptive work if we've lost sight of the way he makes all things new?

Do we know how to walk with *him* in this garden he planted?

Perhaps St. Ignatius, in his commitment to remembering God's nearness, took inspiration from the apostle Paul. In Paul's letter to the Romans, he wrote that God is not hiding, not hard to find. In fact, he has made himself plain, offering himself right here in all that he made: bird and flower, animal, mountain, and human: "What may be known about God is plain . . . because God has made it plain. . . . Since the creation of the world God's invisible qualities—his eternal power and divine nature—have been clearly seen, being understood from what has been made."[9] Richard Rohr describes this revelation of God, saying:

> God always and forever comes as one who is *totally hidden and yet perfectly revealed* in the same moment or event. The first act

> of divine revelation is creation itself. Thus, *nature* is the first Bible, written . . . before the Bible of words.[10]

It is a privilege to open the Bible and learn to read it, study it, find the timeless words of our faith written there for us to receive. And it is a joy, too, to step into this "first Bible," this timeless revelation of God's creative imagination, and cultivate the skills to read it, to accept his invitation and walk with him—and discover that he's been here all along.

New Life Bursting Forth

Margaret Feinberg writes that "God extends endless invitations to encounter him, yet too often we sleep straight through. Unconscious of the life God wants for us, we slumber in the presence of the sacred and snore in the company of the divine. We remain asleep while God roosts in our midst."[11]

The beauty of creation is a great scavenger hunt. Where will I find him roosting today? Where is he hiding in plain sight? With a million extravagances he waves at us, tickling our senses, inviting us to come awake, to come alive, to hear the song and join in the dance. To find him, to behold him. To *be* in his presence.

I don't want to be asleep anymore. I want to be wide awake.

I've found some of the most profound reminders of God's creative presence right at my fingertips, in the chaos and mystery of life itself. The miracle of babies appearing out of nowhere—and the fierce love that emerges from nothing—is an audacious mystery. Life springs forth, beautiful, brand-new, bringing us face-to-face with all we can never fully know. I imagine the Creator rubbing his hands together gleefully, cheering, "See what I did there?"

I do see, and yet, I can't comprehend—and I'm pulled in, drawn up in a desire to see and know him and the creation he is bringing forth right here and now.

How is it that my children, so very alive, so unique and individual, simply did not exist until one fateful night when my actions unwittingly and unknowingly called them into being? How can it be that my own life—so firmly set in reality—began just as tenuously and implausibly? I don't know what baffles and amazes me more: that we exist at all, or that we do not always exist. The two seem mutually exclusive to my finite mind.

But I ponder these things every day, and in doing so, I find myself face-to-face with God—a sacramental beholding.

Years ago, my three-year-old pressed his face against the screen door with a quizzical expression. "I don't know what I did with my scoop," he mused with a tone of real bafflement. It hit me then as it never had before—four years previously, this precious child did not exist. *Did not exist.* Yet there he was, calling on his own distinct will, personality, mannerisms, facial expressions, body language, and tone to tell me that he can't find the gravy ladle that just moments ago he tossed over the porch railing. I was astonished.

My baby was nursing. He was mostly asleep but disturbed by the conversation, and vigilant, ready to bat my hand away should it threaten his personal space and disrupt his peace and quiet. Again, I found myself astonished. One year prior, this tiny babe had not yet been born. Two years earlier, he did not exist. *Did not exist.* And yet there he was, demonstrating a powerful will and body to inform me in no uncertain terms that he will resist should our wills and purposes collide. How can this be?

Sometimes, for just a moment, it hits me that I'm alive, right now, right this very second. I haven't always been, and I won't always be. In fact, my life spans such a tiny, tiny segment of forever. But right now, *right now*, I am here, invited to awaken and behold him *intimately*.

The beauty of life, the invitation of his presence, is so tangible in the bursting forth of newness and spring. So today, I walked among creation and found that in the stillness and thoughtfulness, I walked with him and felt at home—listening, watching, learning. I heard the ground sing as my footprints left marks in the squishy rain-and-snow-soaked ground. I watched a robin sit and warble regally in her tree. I heard a choir of frogs fill their swampy cathedral. I looked at the garbage littered here and there and contemplated that even these intruders will ultimately be returned to nature by the slow processes of nature. I contemplated the rocks towering above me and gasped at the patient work creation does by God's hand—and how our lives are but a breath.

I have beheld you today, in your sanctuary. Your love is

here, so close, better than life. I look at the new life arising all around me, just a hint, barely visible. I wonder what new spark you are kindling within me.

The earth is awakening, and I awaken my soul to you, God.

The soil is being turned and made ready, and I make myself ready for you.

All living things are beginning again. With your strength, I, too, will begin again.

CULTIVATING INTIMACY

Although our Creator is in the beauty and the pain, the joy and the struggle, the flower and the thorn, let's be honest—we often need to practice finding him in the beautiful things before our spiritual "muscles" can see him in the pain and darkness.

Where is beauty in your life today? Perhaps it is the physical beauty of your environment, your family, or an art form you've been admiring. Perhaps it is an intangible beauty in your emotions, thoughts, or relationships. How does this beauty point you to God? How does the art unveil the artist?

A great place to start is the Prayer of Examen, which we can practice anytime of the day:

- **Remind yourself of God's presence.** Step into his light, ask for his eyes to see, remind yourself that he is here.
- **Look around yourself with gratitude.** Give thanks for the details of *this day* and *this moment.*

- **Consider** the feelings, emotions, and thoughts this day has stirred. Invite God into them.
- Reflect on what is wrong, broken, or painful. **Ask for forgiveness, or the strength to forgive, heal, restore.**
- **Look forward** to the coming moments or days. Ask God to remain with you and for a reminder of his presence.

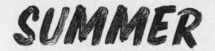

SUMMER

1.
the season between spring and autumn

2.
the warmer half of the year

3.
a period of maturing powers[1]

CHAPTER 4

HEAVENS

Wonder

God is in heaven
and you are on earth,
so let your words be few.

THE TEACHER, ECCLESIASTES 5:2

The best things cannot be told because
they transcend thought.

JOSEPH CAMPBELL, *THE POWER OF MYTH*

MY HUSBAND AND I meander along the Pacific Ocean late at night. It is almost completely dark. Our feet sink into the cool, damp sand as waves roar up and crash around us. The sound is all-consuming, with no visual cues to shrink them back into perspective; I can almost imagine the earth formless, darkness over the surface of the deep, the Spirit of God hovering over the waters.

Turning, we step onto a wooden pier leading far out into the sea. It's a long walk to the end. Stopping now and then to peer down into the water barely visible beneath us, we reach the very edge—a quarter mile into the ocean. Out here, there are no waves crashing against the surf, just an infinity of black waters heaving and rolling as far as the eye can see in any direction.

The sky is a realm of nothingness. No moon shines tonight, and the stars are shrouded by clouds. I cannot locate the place where the waters meet the sky, where the air becomes sea. There is no context, no light, only *out there*, and it goes forever in all directions—up, down, right, and left. Leaning against the rails at the end of the pier, I am both everywhere and nowhere. The sense of being in the vacuum of infinity is so great, I can hardly take a breath. I stand there, tilting, staring into the abyss.

It is terrible, and wonderful.

The story goes that a certain rabbi always kept two pieces of paper on him, one in each pants pocket. In one pocket, the paper read, "For my sake the world was created." In the other pocket, the scrap said, "I am but dust and ashes."[1] Holding both to be true, he reminded himself of each as necessary.

I am great.

I am small.

Here on the precipice between solid and infinity, I sense his point precisely. Some days, I am too caught up in myself, too busy worshiping the daily minutiae of my own life and thoughts to lift my eyes and glimpse transcendence. But at other times, I stand before the wonders of the world helplessly in awe, a wave crashed against the rocks. *I am part of this immense and incredible world, yet entirely at its mercy.*

As a creature in this vast universe, I need these moments of awe, these opportunities to be swept off my feet by a power that can amaze, delight, and destroy. To grapple with something far, far greater than I am. To gaze at someone far more powerful than I can imagine, to explore the truth that I am a speck, vulnerable in every way. To resume a more modest and humble place in the world.

To worship with awe and wonder.

Rendered Speechless

Everyone worships *something*, the old saying goes. If I'm not intentional about laying my heart and hands open before God, I instinctively begin worshiping something else. Too often, this something else is my own self: *my* comfort, plans, ideas, feelings.

But sometimes, the Creator grabs me by the collar, and I'm rendered speechless.

On a hot summer morning, I settle into a coffee shop. This cozy chalet exists to offer small, daily delights—friends, coffee, chocolate croissants. I sip my latte and turn to Facebook. There, at the top of my News Feed, a video demonstrates the most detailed map of the universe we have to date: more than 100,000 galaxies spanning over 500 million light-years.

I am utterly blown away, speechless, spellbound. How can something so massive, so infinitely distant, coexist with me? This computer model immerses me into a place I will never ever see with my tiny, earthbound eyes—but which is no less real for that. Then the demonstration pivots to the impossibly microscopic side of things, the unseen world of atoms too tiny to see—making up every living thing, including the eerily similar-looking universe, the gnats and the trees, the mountains and me.

With the wonder of the Internet, I am gasping at the truly unbelievable size and scale of all things. My latte and I, so real and tangible, are left untouched and speechless.

Walking outside to my car later, I'm still taking it all in: the spider crawling up my leg, branches towering over my head, rocky mountain crags sheltering and imposing. Mere hundreds of light-years away, the stars hang low in the sky. In the face of such enormity, it suddenly seems I have much in common with the spider.

I'm grateful for this chance to worship, to be confronted by all I can never touch, comprehend, or control.

This jolt of awe evokes more than joyous worship, however. There is something akin to terror in acknowledging our place in time and space. How brief our years on earth truly are; how tiny we are in the universe; how powerless we are in the face of might. This world is full of powerful forces ready to sweep us off our feet—sometimes literally.

Living in a major metropolitan area, I lose sight of the dominance that forces of nature hold over creatures like me. We coexist with uncontrollable, unharnessed power. Earthquakes, tornadoes, lightning, and floodwaters—not to mention a hungry, wild predator hunting in the early morning—these are as native to the earth as the ladybugs and daffodils I cherish. It is not only the parts of creation I can hold in my hand that proclaim the truth; those parts that hold *me* provide daily reminders that life is fleeting, that all things are vulnerable. In a vast universe, we are not the center, not royalty; we are the grass of the fields that springs up and withers in a day. In the pecking order of creation, we are not nearly as high as we like to think. Storm winds will topple trees long after I am laid to rest. And long after everything I know has burnt itself out, the volcanoes and earthquakes will go on rumbling and trembling.

But we are loved, with an everlasting love.

With awe flooding my heart, I ask: *Who am I?* We are the most fleeting flower in a garden that constantly ebbs and flows between life and death, tiny creatures whose life is but a breath. Yet God knows us so intimately that even the hairs on our head are numbered.

Tell Me If You Know

On a hot, humid afternoon, my family sits on the porch, listening to the crickets and cicadas, watching the western sky turn from sunny blue to a dark, ominous gray. We are under a severe-weather warning, and we know what is coming: eighty-mile-per-hour winds, tornadoes, softball-sized hail, driving rain. After we stock the basement with candles, radios, and batteries, all we have left to do is wait for it to hit.

In our corner of the world, weather comes from the west. Why check the forecast when you can sit on the front porch? From here, we can see it all. The sky overhead may be bright, but we see the tempest coming. And while the storm rages, a hint of far-off blue along the horizon line promises that all will soon pass.

The storm is intense, as predicted. We hunker down in the basement, the kids shaking while I hold them as a mother hen covers her chicks. Not all the wonders of the world lead to life. Fewer still are calculated to enhance my own little life and needs. The hot, humid weather billows up into destruction—thunderstorms, lightning strikes, devastating tornadoes, storms that utterly destroy.

Confronted by these wonders, these reminders that the world is great and powerful, that we are both part and parcel of the miracle and yet so small and fleeting—this encounter is a terrible, humbling gift. We aren't bombarded by these truths daily, as our ancient brothers and sisters were when they slept outside among the stars and storms or fought for their living among the tenacious prairies, forests, rivers, and mountainsides. Spending our lives shuttling between home, car, and office, we almost entirely miss the reality pulsing all around. We become immune, deaf. We start believing that our tiny, fleeting, anxious ideas are what's most real, valuable, true. We forget to bow before someone greater than ourselves and worship.

Yet when we step outside the mini-malls and interstates, we find ourselves toe-to-toe with the abyss, with the ocean, the mountains, the sky. There is no end of space, of power, of glory, and so little of it is ours or under our control. We are the gnats flying frantically after all, living out a tiny life-span and then gone.

If our transcendent Creator did not come near to us—if he was distant and unreachable—coming face-to-face with the wonders of the universe would be meaningless, or worse, terrifying. But he *is* immanent, walking with me through the forests, sitting with me as the everyday things flow through my fingers. This Creator is both our divine parent and the one who hung the stars and makes the elements dance.

One of the most ancient stories in the Bible is the book of Job, a man who plunged from the heights of wealth and power to the depths of pain and suffering. Immersed in unrelenting pain, Job, his wife, and his friends debate (through poetry!) the most difficult questions of life: suffering, obedience, righteousness, why things are the way they are, and what all this says about God.

Eventually, God interrupts:

Where were you when I laid the earth's foundation?
    Tell me, if you understand.
Who marked off its dimensions? Surely you know!
    Who stretched a measuring line across it?
On what were its footings set,
    or who laid its cornerstone—
while the morning stars sang together
    and all the angels shouted for joy?

Who shut up the sea behind doors
    when it burst forth from the womb,

> when I made the clouds its garment
>   and wrapped it in thick darkness,
> when I fixed limits for it
>   and set its doors and bars in place,
> when I said, "This far you may come and no
>   farther;
>   here is where your proud waves halt"?[2]

The Creator goes on for pages, without answering a single question. In the end, nothing is resolved. None of life's suffering, none of our questions, are explained in a way we can understand.

Let's eavesdrop a bit more on God's "answer":

> Have you ever given orders to the morning,
>   or shown the dawn its place. . . .
>
> What is the way to the abode of light?
>   And where does darkness reside? . . .
>
> Have you entered the storehouses of the snow
>   or seen the storehouses of the hail,
> which I reserve for times of trouble,
>   for days of war and battle? . . .
> Does the rain have a father?
>   Who fathers the drops of dew?
> From whose womb comes the ice?
>   Who gives birth to the frost from the heavens

when the waters become hard as stone,
    when the surface of the deep is frozen? . . .

Who provides food for the raven
    when its young cry out to God
    and wander about for lack of food?

Do you know when the mountain goats give birth?
    Do you watch when the doc bears her fawn?
Do you count the months till they bear?
    Do you know the time they give birth?[3]

No. No, my entire being cries out, *I do not know*. I cannot possibly understand. We are rightly rendered speechless, responding with our brother Job: "*I am unworthy—how can I reply to you? I put my hand over my mouth.*"[4]

Yet somehow, for both Job and me, our speechlessness *is itself* the answer. As we remember that we are but dust and ashes, we arrive at the starting place, where we may accept the invitation to rest in the powerful hands of the one who is eternal. As I remain in this space of awe, my spirit changes. I realize that I am not God, did not give birth to the frost of the heavens, or show the dawn its place. But also, I accept that I am the small, vulnerable creature dearly cared for by the Lord. Like he did with the mountain goat giving birth, the doe with her fawn, the young raven crying out for food—God meets us in our smallness. God, the Mighty One, knows our names!

He comes to us, even in times of grief, and feeds us—body, spirit, and soul.

In the thousands of years since Job and his friends argued over the meaning of deep suffering, millions more have shouted their grief-drenched questions to the sky. These vulnerable requests for understanding have never been resolved as fully as we would like.

But God has spoken, is always speaking. In our suffering, doubting, and queries, he replies, as he did to Job, with his presence, power, and sovereignty. God startles us awake with majesty and overtakes us with awe and wonder. For from him, and through him, and to him are all things. None of the marvels of creation were begun at my command, nor are they here to please or serve me. We are small, and yet we rest inside his almighty hand. The one who gives orders to the morning is the one who sustains us in life and receives us in death.

I, too, have shouted unfathomable questions at the sky, refusing to be silent until my petitions have been met—but all my divine contracts are returned to me, unsigned. The peace I find is not in the answers I demand but in laying them down, in laying *myself* down. In kneeling, bowing, falling on my face and surrendering to the one who knows the way to the abode of light.

This comfort is not what we asked for, but often it *is* what we need. We were made to find peace in adoring him; after all, our hearts are restless until we rest in him.[5]

Is this enough for us, for you? As the waves crash, and the

mountains shake, and the sky darkens, can we surrender in worship to a power who is infinitely greater than we?

We are vulnerable and small, yes. But he loves us and cares for us as his own. We can release ourselves into his infinite hands. We *need* to. Like an infant child carried by a strong parent, we can find relief in our smallness, for the one who laid the earth's foundations considers us precious enough to call us his own.

Eclipsed

The day was hot. The last I'd checked, 100 degrees and 108 with the heat index. We'd tried hiking through the forests and prairies to pass the time, exploring the Mississippi River, where we'd settled. But the heat sapped our strength. Instead, we sat around panting, trying to play cards, rationing water and snacks. Waiting.

Even with the heat, we waited in the sun, of course. There was no point looking for shade. The sun is what we had come to see.

The five of us—me, my husband, and three children—had driven six hours south to see the total solar eclipse. We were promised seventeen seconds of totality from our hotel parking lot, but we wanted more. That's how we ended up at this park along the Mississippi, in time to snatch up one of the few parking spots available and begin our wait.

Since our arrival, the weather had gotten hotter, the sky brighter. More and more people arrived, with solar glasses and telescopes and huge expensive cameras. Everyone was set up and waiting, chatting with each other, sharing extra glasses, advice, and peeks through fancy equipment. In a country so tense and torn, we were a crowd of strangers easily recognizing each other as neighbors. We had a shared goal, a common hope. We would succeed or fail together.

I glanced at the time: 11:45 a.m. “It’s starting,” I told my sweaty, cranky children.

We grabbed our devices—pinhole paper plates, cereal-box viewers, solar glasses—and tried each one in turns. Sure enough, there was a small sliver eating away at the sun.

For another ninety minutes, we continued the vigil, trying to stay cool, peeking occasionally at the progress, chatting with the others. There was so much to take in. A violinist serenading his elderly mother. A woman with eclipse tattoos spanning the entire length of her back. A family with three types of high-tech telescopes, more than willing to let hundreds of us peek through occasionally. The leaf and tree shadows falling as half-moons on the sidewalk.

And then, as so many long-awaited things approach, everything was suddenly tumbling forward, moving so fast toward completion after such a long wait. Now the temperature was comfortable and cool, the view around me strangely dim.

Checking the clock again, I whispered to my kids: ten more minutes.

Cloaked in protective glasses, we stared at the sun. The

sliver became smaller and smaller . . . then was gone. Entirely gone.

We dropped our glasses to the ground, staring at the hole in the sky with our bare eyes. It was jarring—physically, emotionally, spiritually, *viscerally*—to watch our own sun, the source of all life on earth, dissipate into nothing at midday, at its zenith. The warmth, the light, even the thing itself, was entirely gone.

There was far, far too much happening to take it all in. Stars broke out around me, as sunset colors appeared along the full 360-degree horizon. The air became dark and chill, rattling with the noise of evening bugs coming awake in the prairie grasses and trees. I kissed my husband, jumped up and down with my kids. I stared at the corona, at the brilliant, sparking diamond-ring effect.

It was a wonder like nothing else on this earth, two fleeting minutes utterly unlike all other minutes.

All around us, strangers were enveloped in the same spontaneous, unbridled emotion, without self-consciousness, without boundaries. Naked joy and emotion overflowed on every face, voice, and body around me, each of us confronted with the certainty that we are so very small in such a vast and uncontrollable universe.

And then, bursting forth, the sun exploded brilliantly, victoriously. It was finished. With sudden sunrise, the world sprang back to normal life again. The colors faded from the horizon, the birds and bugs quieted, and slowly, slowly, the blinding brightness and heat returned.

We put glasses on again, watching the sun creep back into place. One by one, our companions packed up their cameras and blankets and coolers and cars.

And then we left, all of us. The tiny country park became countryside again. Back to the world as we know it, as we figured it had always been and always would be.

The trip home that evening lasted an eternity. Crawling in long parades of wonder-stuck travelers through cornfields and country towns at twenty miles an hour, my children faced the long evening with equanimity and audio books. I asked what they thought of the day. "Awesome," they said. "Amazing." "We have no words to describe it," they said, then sputtered gibberish to prove their point.

Later that night, I watched the eclipse from the perspective of NASA's satellites: our Earth, our continent, with a giant shadow of darkness spreading over us, creeping, covering all of us. This terrifying wonder swept across our nation, from sea to shining sea. But to those of us who stood in the dark, it was not a terrifying, crawling shadow but a gift, a once-in-a-lifetime invitation to stand with strangers and look boldly into the sun, to see life improbably upside down for exactly two minutes.

At the end of this day, no profound object lesson is needed, or even possible, for mere words cannot depict the truth embedded within these moments of awe and wonder. Isn't that what language is, after all: our limited but ever-expanding attempts to convey what we have seen and must, somehow, find a way to share?

Tomorrow, we will go back to the millions of things required to make a life, a thousand small tasks that must be done. It will be harder to remember, to seek out those glimpses of eternity that put me, gloriously, in my place—small in a vast world, yet dearly and intimately loved by the powerful creator of all things. Still, today our cups have been filled with wonder, and we carry the lesson home in our spirits. Today, the awe of witnessing creation is more than enough.

Indeed, we *are* great and small.

CULTIVATING WONDER

It can be all too easy to lose sight of wonder as we go about our daily lives, to lose the capacity for awe. And yet, the wonder-full and awe-some are all around us. How can we come awake to it, and to him?

- Accept the advice of the rabbi and **make two statements**: "For my sake the world was created" and "I am but dust and ashes." Or if carrying slips of paper around isn't your thing, find another way to remember. Perhaps hang contrasting pictures on the wall or write the quotes on your desktop. Which of these do you tend to remember, and which do you tend to forget? Look for ways to live within, and celebrate, the tension of both.

- **Keep your eyes open to wonder and awe** in your daily life. What things are beyond your comprehension and control? Go outside in the middle of the night and look at the stars. Stand on the porch in the middle of a storm and watch the power of wind and lightning go by. Walk by the ocean and let the crashing waves silence your cluttered thoughts. Take a moment to look and listen to these things and truly see and hear them.

- **Worship** the God who is near and yet transcendent, whom we know and yet can never fully understand. Bow down before him—literally, if you can!—and acknowledge that he is far, far beyond our understanding. Allow these moments of silence before God to heal your spirit, like a child resting safely in a loving parent's arms.

CHAPTER 5

ABUNDANCE

Purpose

Only while you are alive is there hope of finding Him.

KABIR, "THE SWING OF CONSCIOUSNESS"

If God had wanted to be a big secret, He would not have created babbling brooks and whispering pines.

ROBERT BRAULT, *ROUND UP THE USUAL SUBJECTS*

I STEP OUTSIDE to call my children: *Time to stop playing and get in the car!* Ten minutes ago, I sent them out, washed and dressed, so I could finalize the last-minute details for today's family party.

A rookie mistake, obviously.

As they streak past me, I notice that something has gone very, very wrong. My darling daughter's face, neck, hands, and sundress are streaked with raspberry juice. And my son—oh my abundant-life son—has covered his entire head with mud. Literally the only thing I can see are his bright and shining eyes.

I scream for everyone to stop. They freeze, caked hands

clutching door handles. Texting my parents to apologize for what I'm confident will be a lengthy delay, I gingerly place a child under each arm and head for the shower.

I can't be mad. I can't be anything other than shaking with laughter. What is summer if not dripping with delights, imploring us to get our hands dirty, inviting us to immerse our faces in the abundance and relish the richness of it all? Why are we on earth if not to dive right in? My children were merely flourishing, answering the call of life as they were made to do.

Cacophony

Here is the wild paradox of creation: God ordered the world out of chaos, but the verdancy of life results in a whole new kind of chaos. Clearly, God's purpose in organizing a formless void into millipedes, jellyfish, hedgehogs, and poison ivy was not so we could sit restfully in a meditative state. We stubbornly hope that life will leave us more or less alone in peace and quiet, that the forces of nature and human nature will be straightforward and controllable, bending to our own dictation. But life exists only inside messy, colliding relationships. From the sperm and the egg, the bee and the pollen, life is about crashing into each other—for better or for worse (and most of the time, a good bit of both).

We celebrate that God made order and form out of emptiness, but there's another angle to consider. God had an eternity of time in which he alone existed, in triune unity. Can you imagine the harmony? Why mess that up with a garden? I can exhibit a great deal of love, peace, and self-control when I'm in a room by myself, as long as you don't introduce anyone else into the picture. What was it like when God and God alone reigned in the vacuum of unformed reality?

But this peace and quiet, this overflowing of goodness and righteousness was not, apparently, the ambiance God was going for. While it may sound heavenly to me, harmonious solitude is not what our Creator pronounced *good.* God decided to mix things up in a major way.

As we have seen, the Creator is a gardener. Like my son, he gets his hands dirty. The story told in Genesis 2 depicts God planting purposely, beginning a world swarming with life. Into this story, God adds a human, living alone in God's presence. Again, I wonder: Why mess this up? So nice, just the two of them in paradise. Yet in God's creative scheme, one is not enough for the collisions necessary for abundance. God creates a second human—and still, the resulting chaos isn't enough. He orders the two to increase, to multiply, to make more and more and more life. More noise, more chaos, more crashing and colliding, more cacophony.

It seems that God thrives and rejoices in the pandemonium of living things bumping constantly against each other—and believes that we do too. Anyone who has attempted living both alone and in a crowded household knows that much fulfillment come out of relationships, but also a great deal of clamor and crazy. We flourish through jumping into the crazy, by surrounding ourselves with creation and burgeoning abundance.

This isn't how we want to picture goodness, most of us. We don't like the constant jostling and treading on feet, don't want to be tripped up by crowds, nibbled by gnats, bombarded by smells, harangued by noise. We'd like to think that real goodness, godliness even, lies in the silence, the solitude, the ordered, clean, and controlled. But our Creator doesn't seem to agree. Everything about what he made is *alive*, teeming and swarming and crawling and howling. The only alternative to abundance is death.

Life is where he is. In the towering storms and bubbling brooks, in the crying babies and chatty neighbors, in the watermelon juice dribbling off our chins, in the scuttling chipmunks and soaring dolphins. This crazy, abundant bombardment of sights and smells and sounds is where he delights, where he hangs out, where we can find him.

He is present not only in prayer and meditation rooms but also in the dense fertility of life crashing everywhere.

Living on Purpose

Summer is the height of extremes. Gone is the subtlety of spring with its pastel colors, mild temperatures, and tiny beginnings. Here instead comes the vibrancy of summer—bold colors, loud noises, overindulgences, exaggerations, and excesses everywhere. The sun burns hot, the rain falls hard, the winds drive violently.

We simply must immerse ourselves in summer's vibrancy, richness, and fullness. We wade knee-deep through glorious riverbeds, chasing frogs and fish and snakes. We climb trees, hike trails, paddle a boat into the middle of nowhere, down a cool glass of lemonade in one long, refreshing drink, sink our teeth into an exquisitely juicy nectarine. Summer is the chocolate of the seasons—a perfectly shaped blackberry, almost too delicious to be true.

Every corner of the world teems now with life and busyness. Every surface crawls with bugs, every breath of wind carries the seeds of a million different organisms. Even the moisture in the air seems determined to launch colonies of mold or mildew on every surface it finds. Every inch of space—solid, liquid, or air—swarms with infinite life, flinging out its limbs to holler, "I am aliiiiive!"

Everywhere, everywhere is abundance, flourishing, delight—all colliding at once. Watermelons, peaches, and ice-cream cones drip with sweet nectar, rolling down our chins and arms, creating sticky hands and hair. Walking through the pungent grass, we disturb entire colonies of creatures; growing weeds and grasses scratch bare legs, tiny bugs and creatures crawl up our shorts and nibble elbows when we sit down. If you take a shovel to the dark, hot soil, you'll find the earth simmering with life—every scoop wiggling with worms and slugs and bacteria so small you can't see them.

None of this abundance sits still, just watching the day go by. Children run and play, getting muddy and sunburned and strong. Animals dig, build, eat, and store. Bugs flit around, carrying and planting and fertilizing. Butterflies and bees dart everywhere, doing their thing. Plants grow unstoppable, bursting through cement and under fences, as thick and fast as a jungle. All of creation is actualized now, demonstrating extravagantly that it exists for a purpose.

The word *purpose* sounds boring, grownup, and lifeless; corporate branding and self-help books have squeezed the meaning from it entirely. But there is nothing boring and lifeless about living on purpose. Our Creator fashioned jungles, prairies, puppies, and people for a reason, with intent. He has a goal in mind. And in these seasons of flourishing, he forms us toward this purpose like a growth spurt.

As for us, we long for meaning deep in our bodies, minds, and souls. Significance draws us like a magnet. We crave confirmation that we're more than accidents taking up space, intended for more than surviving a span of time before death, that our life's energy is as needful and purposeful as the blazing sun and buzzing bees of summer. The whole point of beginning and becoming is the adventure of living into our purpose.

In philosophy and theology there is a concept called *telos*, a Greek word that means "end purpose" or "goal." Mark McMinn describes telos like this:

> If we could imagine a fully whole human living a thriving, abundant life, then we would be picturing something like telos. . . . [Telos is] about finding the natural and purposeful end of what it means to be fully human. An acorn grows into

> a majestic oak tree and finds its telos, and a human may grow into a fully functioning person, revealing what humans are for.[1]

This season of flourishing, of abundance, demonstrates telos vividly, as all living things dash toward becoming. Life in this moment is unstoppable, overflowing all boundaries. We can hardly rein it in. Life has it in mind to take over completely. This is not the time to wait around, to see what happens. Make every moment count. Now is the time to get up and *go for it.*

Growing

Of course, the haunting question for many of us is . . . go for *what*? Without a clear view of what flourishing in telos looks like, we're as restless as a child scratching mosquito bites on a humid summer evening. Sometimes purpose is easy to see. Take the vines in my garden, for instance. Give these raised beds a day or two to themselves, and they're beyond my ability to intervene—tomato stalks shoot so high they fall over, weighed down by fruit and flowers. They live and move and have their being inside the Creator and his plan. They don't need to search out one single purpose for their time on earth, for their path forward is clear: spring up, produce fruit in abundance, wither and fall. In simply *being*, they do exactly what God created them to do.

Similarly, I know what growing toward telos looks like for the baby birds taking their first flights across my yard, dogged (literally) by my overeager watchdog puppy. I understand what it looks like for these infant robins to become fully what they were made to be. I can look at an acorn and see the mighty oak it is destined to become, as McMinn describes.

But what about you and me? What is *our* end goal, the ultimate purpose he prunes and cultivates us toward? What are *we* meant to grow into during these growth spurts?

So much of our formative years are spent on education, careers, social status—important things if we are to survive in this world and provide for our families. But wisdom reminds us that there is so much more we are meant to become. Micah 6:8 summarizes it nicely:

> O people, the Lord has told you what is good,
> and this is what he requires of you:
> to do what is right, to love mercy,
> and to walk humbly with your God.[2]

Or as Paul says in his own summary, the fruit of the Spirit is "love, joy, peace, patience, kindness, goodness, faithfulness, gentleness, and self-control."[3]

This fruit doesn't grow effortlessly, at least not in my life. If left untended, I'd be a garden bed tangled with self-centeredness, worry, greed, and cynicism. It's a huge project to pull these weeds, day after day. They're deeply rooted and fast growing, and meanwhile, I must plant love and joy, cultivate peace and patience, nurture kindness and goodness. It sounds so easy to "do what is right, to love mercy, and to walk humbly," but practically speaking, this is the challenge of our lives. Caring for people I consider enemies takes a great deal of effort, as does being generous with those I find undeserving, choosing my words carefully, moving outside my comfort zone, setting aside my privilege, giving sacrificially—to name just a few.

Becoming takes an abundance of persistent cultivation.

Fortunately, growing in love and mercy and faithfulness can be habit-forming. We cultivate and nurture what is right and good not only to grow toward flourishing but because we begin delighting in the fruit—and sometimes, even in the work itself. After all, who doesn't love a handful of fresh summer raspberries? The reward of pruning back the thorns is well worth the effort.

The catechism asks, "What is the chief end of man?" and famously answers, "To glorify God and enjoy him forever."[4] Can you imagine a world where humans grow eagerly into this destiny—into righteousness, mercy, humility, love, joy, peace, patience, kindness, goodness, faithfulness, gentleness, self-control, and above all, glorifying God—and find that we enjoy it enough to go on doing so forever?

Abundant Life

God has a telos too; a purpose, an end goal in sight. He has begun with the end in mind. Our living-and-active Creator continues to work this garden, pruning and nurturing all life toward redemption, wholeness, shalom.

Jesus didn't mention the word *telos* as far as I know, but he taught his followers that he came to bring life, *abundant* life.[5] Christians have never fully agreed on what Jesus meant by that (do we fully agree on anything, really?). But if we look at what else he said, the way he lived his own life and how it ended, it seems clear that Jesus isn't promising health, wealth, and happiness flowing and overflowing in and out of season. After all, Jesus had no place of his own to lay his head. He wept, sweated drops of blood, was abandoned and betrayed by his closest friends, and was murdered in the most vicious way possible. But through all these hardships, he brought abundant life—and it proved too tenacious even for death.

The meaning and purpose we so deeply long for is found in chasing our telos of right-living, delighting in the Creator and the cacophony of his creation along the way. And in doing so, we participate in cultivating shalom for all creation. After all, the Creator formed us from the quiet peacefulness of dust and invited us to live life to the full, to make our chief goal delighting in him.

In the summertime season, so full of doing, tasting, running, and living, so packed with life and its pleasures, take time to sit and drink it all in, to smell the neighbor's grill, to doze in the garden, to feel the cool grass or the hot sand under your toes—to delight in the abundance of abundant life. There are lessons to learn that have no words, and we must breathe them in, letting go and allowing them to wrap around us, allowing ourselves to flourish through delight.

May you feel today, at least for a second, the ostentatious

delight of the unbelievable truth that God enjoys you, too—created you *for the purpose of enjoying you.* Enjoys you like the glasses of cold lemonade and ice-cream cones of summer. Enjoys you like a run through the dew-drenched grass or the smell of fresh-cut flowers or the taste of a garden-plucked tomato.

He invites you, in all these things, to find your own purpose in enjoying him forever.

Life is thick with chaos and cacophony, struggle and storm. But also, the evening sun streaming through forest branches, pooling in the prairie flowers.

And then, when it sets, fireflies.

CULTIVATING PURPOSE

What parts of God's creation do you love to taste, to delight in? God is in all these things, and we can use them as pointers teaching us how to see him, pathways to worship *him*. You, too, are part of this good, abundant creation. How is he forming you today? What are you growing into?

- **Take a moment to taste** something. Really relish it, noticing the textures and flavors and smells. Thank God for his creativity, the delightful way he provides nourishment, beauty, and enjoyment all in one.
- **Consider** what kind of fruit your life is cultivating now. What sort of telos are you heading toward—is this the direction you want to be heading? What small adjustments could you make?

- **Take some time to sit** in the cacophony that fills your life in this season. Acknowledge that God is in these places too. Ask him to reveal himself to you even in the chaos.

CHAPTER 6

TOIL

Faithfulness

The God whom I know dwells quietly in the root system of the very nature of things.

PARKER J. PALMER, *LET YOUR LIFE SPEAK*

Ambitious people climb, but faithful people build.

JULIA WARD HOWE, *THE WALK WITH GOD*

ON A HOT SUMMER afternoon, I'm at the pool, smearing sunscreen on my squirming child's face, expertly avoiding her eyes while never taking *my* eyes off the other two children in the water. Let me tell you: If there's anywhere adulthood fails to live up to the brochures, it's poolside.

Looking around the deck, I notice that we swimmers are broken into two groups. At the deep end, teens and twenty-somethings cluster in pairs of twos and fours, while in the shallows, parents, grandparents, and aunties surround babies, toddlers, and preschoolers. Each side models vastly different swimming suits, some showcasing strong and beautiful bodies, others chosen for practical material carefully constructed to keep everything in place while chasing toddlers, tossing preschoolers into the water, and nursing babies (often all at once). At the deep end, everyone entangles themselves, flirting, laughing, splashing. The shallow end of the pool has a great deal of laughing and splashing too, but more *disentangling* from small children while keeping everyone alive, protected from the sun, and filled with enough snacks and drinks to avert disaster.

One of these groups looks casual and carefree. The other looks a bit hassled and harassed.

Although these two displays of "swimming" appear as different as night and day, I know for certain that one leads directly to the other. At least for some, the carefree flirtations at the deep end result in the inflatable floaties and SPF 50 at the shallow end.

All this is by design, of course: The fun and energy of new life evolves naturally into the duties and exhaustion of adulthood.

Cultivate and Keep

In the cacophony of life we've been relishing, the delights are endless—as is the work, the labor, the ongoing maintenance. This garden grows a bit unruly and needs so much care.

So many things need doing all at once. The sun accommodates as best it can, rising early and setting late. There are gardens to weed, ball games to play, lawns to mow, lakes to splash in, barbeques and bonfires to light, picnics to organize. This month, a crisis sprang up at my office, and I've been called in to work long hours. Family birthdays, recitals, and doctor appointments cram the family calendar for the next several weeks. Appointments and deadlines peek around every corner, and the piles of papers waiting for me to sort, sign, and return have reached fire-hazard status. This is my garden, the patch of life and community for which I'm responsible. It's a bit overgrown, yes, and the only way to cut it back is to put on a pair of sturdy shoes and get to work.

There's always something on the urgent list. We're responsible for feeding, warming, and sustaining ourselves and our families, investing in our communities, contributing to the flourishing of the earth for the sake of generations to come. It is our turn to stay the course, to persevere. From the joys and delights flow the duty; from the labor and work flow the pleasures. The two are not opposites, but side-by-side, intermingled, tumbling through time entangled by faithfulness.

We don't need a special commandment or sacred story to prove any of this: Our own lived experience is proof enough. We are hungry and cold, so we work. Period.

And yet, a story is given to us. After the Gardener finished his careful planting, he took the person formed from clay and placed him in the Garden "to work it and take care of it."[1] Other translations describe this vocation as "tend and watch over" or "cultivate and keep."[2] Whatever words you prefer, the storyteller's point is clear: Our reason for being here, at least in part, is to partner with God in cultivating and caring for the earth. We create the present and future alongside him, partaking in both the labor and the delights. Our duty is to protect and provide, to pour out the energy of our life. Though such work never comes with an official position description, title, or salary, our children, parents, grandparents, siblings, and neighbors need tending. There is no corner of the universe that is outside our zone of accountability. We must take care of each other. This is part and parcel of the original "very good" design.

Even in the most menial-seeming tasks of daily living—dishes, toilets, laundry—our steadfast efforts create life and living for ourselves and those who lean on us. The demands of perseverance may not allow for the time or energy to reflect on any of this, to look around and notice the garden of life our unending labor produces, but it's true all the same. There is creation here, life-giving, like ice water on a hot day. My body and mind are weary, there is so little freedom or time to spare; but as we continue faithfully bending our backs, side by side, the fruit of our labors is *life*.

Toil and Trouble

My friend calls me on the phone: She feels called to ministry, and the doors of opportunity have finally opened wide. But she's been diagnosed with a degenerative illness and can't get out of bed. Another friend works long, long hours at a job he hates—but because he does, his children have good health insurance. My community gathers around one of our own, who can't figure out if she should leave her husband, finally, or dig in and find a way to stay.

Somehow, we expect life to be easier than it is. We picture a joyful experience, occasionally dipping down through setbacks—manageable ones like broken sewer pipes or a bout with the common cold—just as often soaring through the heights of success and vacations and fulfillment. Yet reality seems much more erratic. Life is hard, *bona fide* hard. We work until our strength gives out, but responsibilities still nip at our heels. We fight through hard relationships, dead-end jobs, cancer diagnoses, unhappy endings. Even holidays and vacations are scattered with conflict and disappointment. What feels like a temporary dip becomes the norm.

Why is life so depleting, when we want so badly for it to be satisfying? Faithfulness in the small-but-joyful minutiae of everyday living is one thing; faithfulness through years of darkness requires a different set of muscles entirely.

There's a growing buzz these days that adulthood should include less duty, more living to please ourselves. Let's throw off the shackles of cultural expectations and do what feels good, not what we're told we must do—or so these voices recommend. There's value in overthrowing outdated expectations, but we'll never find the freedom we want in living primarily for ourselves. As Leslie Leyland Fields asks, "Is [living for myself] really all there is? Did we survive childhood, adolescence, and our twenties and thirties to arrive on the doorstep we left as children? Surely not."[3]

Grown-ups leave the party early and go to bed because

work starts at 7:00 a.m. We get up in the middle of the night when we're sick because the baby is crying. We turn down a dream job because weekly travel isn't possible while caring for a terminally ill family member. We do what we must do. Or as my husband likes to say, "We must learn to do what we do not want to do."

Somewhere around the middle, life becomes overwhelming, untenable. Must I live with these people *for the rest of my life*? Will this disease make getting out of bed each day painful *until I die*? The years ahead pile up in a dizzying way when we think about the cycles of pain and frustration we're so eager to break. Our society doesn't put much value in doing the right thing, every day, faithfully, without reward. We're more interested in #livingmybestlifenow and #followingmytruth.

At a younger, earlier time, we laid out our hopes and hearts into the vulnerable universe without any assurance of reward. Now, we pour out the energy of our one-and-only life—still with no guarantees.

Still, faithfulness beckons. A prudent, discerning faithfulness sorts through unreasonable expectations and long-term commitments to discover what to discard, what to repurpose, and where to stay the course. Perseverance always believes there is a light at the end of the tunnel, a prize worth receiving at the finish line.

Who can offer wise advice in these middle years of duty when our weary spirits cry out, depleted? How do we know when to put our needs aside and dig deep, and when we should take the airline's advice and grab our own oxygen mask first?[4] Thankfully, faithfulness is a team sport. We were never meant to figure it all out alone.

Love Your Neighbor

Several years ago, I was pregnant with my third child and in the middle of a move. This required packing and transferring a household from one place to another with two toddler boys in tow. The trouble was, I couldn't stand up for more than a minute or two without running to the bathroom (thanks, morning sickness). Progress was slow, to say the least.

One Sunday morning, my husband ran into a woman he hardly knew in our church hallway. Making small talk, she asked how we were doing—and he answered honestly. It was a brief chat with a near stranger. But she took the information to her Sunday school class full of recently retired adults. A group of them showed up the next morning, packed up half of our apartment, and left hand-me-down bicycles for my boys.

For this faithful group, I was a neighbor—not because of where I lived or how we were related, but simply because I was in need. They poured themselves out to serve me.

This is the ongoing circle of faithfulness: We hold each other up when we think we can't go on. We give of ourselves not only to meet our own needs but also to create life for others. And these others keep us going in turn, bringing us meals during a crisis, offering prayer and guidance during tough decisions, sitting with us while we cry in times of grief—being together, in all seasons. Physically, emotionally, spiritually—the load is too heavy for any one of us to bear. But when we look out for each other, taking on each other's burdens, the load becomes lighter. We can make it, together. When we all share the weight, there is strength enough—and joy abounds within the labors as well.

This isn't just a happy coincidence, a convenient symbiosis. The interdependence cultivated between people during seasons of toil and faithfulness is exactly what God intended when he made this world and invited us to create alongside him.

The book of Revelation, the final book of the Bible, is a challenging read in a genre we don't use or understand much these days. But I love the letters to the churches. A powerful and unambiguous theme emerges: *You all, stay the course. Be faithful. He is coming! He is coming! Keep standing together! Stand firm. Stand, stand, stand. He is coming.*

I had no idea, earlier in life, just how hard it was to stay faithful for the long haul, to maintain "a long obedience in the same direction," as Eugene Peterson says.[5] Exhaustion kicks in miles before the race is over. We can't remember why we're on this path in the first place and begin to wonder what would happen if we just bowed out.

There is a reason the letters in Revelation are written to churches, not individual people: We cannot succeed in faithfulness on our own. Alone, striving to be the legendary lone-ranger hero, we will be lost. Life is a group project from first to last. And so, we join the community of God and take our vows together with these brave and ancient words: "We will, with God's help."[6]

The Pharisees and Sadducees were tag-teaming, taking turns trying to stump Jesus and trap him in trick questions. Then a law expert came forward and asked, "Which is the greatest commandment?"[7]

This cracks me up. It's like the lawyer got nervous and blanked. Or maybe he lobbed a pitch instead of throwing a curveball because he actually wanted Jesus to win . . . but couldn't afford to let on. In any case, Jesus easily clears the hurdle by quoting the Shema, the centerpiece of Jewish thought and worship.[8] Taken from Deuteronomy 6, it begins, "Hear, O Israel: The Lord our God, the Lord is one. Love the Lord your God with all your heart and with all your soul and with all your strength."[9]

The word we translate "strength" in Deuteronomy could be better rendered "muchness." It doesn't just mean physical or mental power, it means to love him *exceedingly* or *abundantly.* Love God much-ly. *This*, Jesus confirms, is our primary duty, our greatest task in life. It is from here that all other duties stem. Faithfulness is found in loving God abundantly: with all our heart, and all our soul, and all our *muchness.*[10] If we remain faithful to this love, like a branch grafted securely to the strong, life-giving vine, we will live.

And then Jesus continues, adding the second-greatest commandment: "Love your neighbor as yourself."[11]

The older I get, the more I realize how profound this call-to-life is. Embodying abundant love is not a check-the-box sort of thing: *Love-feelings for God? Check! Affection for neighbor? Check-check!* Muchness toward God and neighbors requires dug-in faithfulness through the long haul, through thick and thin, better or worse.

If we lived in perpetual winter, I doubt I would ever get to know the people who live around me. But in summer, we all come outdoors, sharing swing sets and soccer balls, mowing each other's lawns, offering excess zucchini, stopping to chat on walks around the block. We need this connection to neighbors—and the responsibility that goes with it. Humans were not created as islands, but as families, tribes, communities. We know, and become, and grow *together.* We are interdependent with neighbors in all their varieties—those across the street and, in today's global village, across the world.

Neighbors come in all shapes and sizes, some of whom you wouldn't expect. When Jesus said that one of the greatest commandments is to love your neighbor, the tricky questions got tougher: "Who is my neighbor?" someone asked. Instead of pointing to the house next door, Jesus launched, characteristically, into a meandering story of a man in desperate need of help. The people considered righteous couldn't be bothered to lend a hand, but a person considered lowborn and detestable sacrificially poured out his time, money, and safety to see this man back to health.

"Which of these men was a neighbor?" Jesus asked.[12] Cleary, the neighbor we are meant to love is whomever we encounter who needs a hand. And the person to whom we reach out ourselves when we cannot go another step.

Burnt Out

During another hot July, my family took a road trip to my beautiful home state of Minnesota. Here in lake country, green things grow like a jungle. Bugs nibble us, allergies goad my skin, and sweat rolls down the small of my back. Leaving the swarms of mosquitoes and gnats at the shore, I spend every second I can at the center of Minnesota's ten thousand lakes. Here in the silence, I breathe in the humid air and search out the haunting cries of my favorite nonhuman creature, the common loon. The respite I crave most waits here among the quiet waters.

One day, we leave the lake and hike through the forest to the headwaters of the Mississippi. Emerging from the woods, we see it: a tiny stream flowing from the glacial Lake Itasca. We take pictures of ourselves leaping across the Mississippi River, this great and mighty body of water at its infancy. The kids and I begin at the beginning, walking down the river like giants, covered only to our knees. We pretend that we intend to travel the entire length; as we hike, the water rises to my thighs, then my waist. I pull the kids onto my back and my hips, and we continue, down, down through this tiny stream that is the mighty Mississippi.

It begins small, as all things do, but—mile by mile—grows and expands, becoming one of the world's greatest water systems, creating life and habitat for countless species. But it all originates here at the source. None of its majesty and power and life-giving would be possible if Lake Itasca, the primary source of this great river, dried up in the heat of summer.

We, too, start small, then grow until we lose sight of where we began, and why, overtaken by the obligations demanding our daily attention. And we, too, will run dry if we disconnect from the source.

Summer is full of color, bursting forth everywhere with bold greens and reds and blues, fireworks and warm tomatoes. But a great deal of energy is required to maintain all this life and living. After a few short months, late summer is burnt out. Leaves and grass look singed, brown, lagging, weary. There has been so much activity, so much growth, so much life. Late summer is exhausted.

I feel burnt out too. This season of pouring out is relentless, pulling at me from all sides. Things aren't turning out the way they do in the movies. We all knew life wasn't a fairy tale, and we didn't *really* expect it to be. But adult life—and not just at the pool—doesn't match up to the brochures. Marriage and parenting are more complicated and painful and less controllable than in the seminars and books. The opposite scenarios—living alone, infertility, or childlessness—can be even more daunting. Work is often just that: work. Opportunities we thought would materialize evaporate, unrealized. The decades pass by far more quickly than we dreamed possible. Life, with all its pleasures, can feel like shouldering responsibilities, sorting stacks of mail, and trying to make ends meet—world without end.

But our task now is to stay firm. God is here, as is the community of Christ, bearing the load alongside us always. In the repetition of toil, in the interplay of coming alongside each other to give and receive support, the seeds of faithfulness germinate within us. One day, one responsibility at a time.

Friends, we have so many duties to bear and responsibilities to carry as we take our turn creating life. But our God is here, working alongside us, working *on us* as we grow, as we give him our years of energy and abundance.

May God's presence strengthen you for the work that lies ahead. And may we find that *his* strength is enough to see us faithfully through to the end of all our labors.

CULTIVATING FAITHFULNESS

Where are you feeling the weight of responsibility in your life? Perhaps you are keeping your nose to the grindstone to provide for your family or continuing through painful treatments to fight off a disease. You may be laboring to nurture infants or care for aging parents. Or perhaps the singular task of staying faithful over time has just become a hard path to travel.

Our Creator is here, too, on these long walks of duty. It is his strength that keeps us going and ultimately brings us to the finish line. How can you find him, here?

- **Make a list** of the responsibilities you carry in this season and turn it into a spiritual checkup. Which are joyful? Which are wearing you down? How does each create life for someone, somehow? Are there some that you should (and could) let go?
- As you work, **remember** that God created us to work alongside him, that laboring can be one of his good gifts, producing life and joy. Find a visual image of God at work, and place it where you can see it as you work alongside him.
- **Ask God**, directly, daily, unrelentingly: *Where are you in these tasks? How can I serve you here, find you here, rest in you here, know you here?*
- Explore ways to **stay connected to the source** of strength. Take five-minute breaks when you can. Step outside and breathe deeply of fresh air. Sit down and enjoy your favorite beverage. Play worship music and invite God into this moment. Set a reminder on your phone to whisper prayers throughout the day.

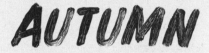

AUTUMN

1.

the season between summer and winter . . .
called also fall

2.

a period of maturity or incipient decline

3.

the later part of someone's life or of
something's existence[1]

CHAPTER 7

HARVEST

Gratitude

The true harvest of my life is intangible—a little star dust caught, a portion of the rainbow I have clutched.

HENRY DAVID THOREAU, *WALDEN*

Of autumn's wine, now drink your fill; the frost's on the pumpkin, and snow's on the hill.

THE OLD FARMER'S ALMANAC, 1993

TIME MARCHES ON, as it always does. The demanding days of summer, bursting with life and busyness, wind down and cool down and settle down into autumn. Harvest is a season of bounty, of rejoicing in the fruits of our labors, a window to reflect on all we have fashioned through our efforts.

My friends go crazy for the first glimpse of autumn. Cool weather! Cozy sweaters! *Pumpkin spice lattes!* (Confession: I've never tried one.) As my son once declared, "It's not hot, it's not cold—it's sweater weather!" School starts up again, which means brand-new notebooks and crayons, a new pair of jeans. The first-day-of-school lineup outside our elementary building has the highest concentration of clean tennis shoes anywhere in the world.

There's a sense of deep-relief-tinged-with-excitement in early autumn. Oppressive heat, sunburns, and mosquitoes have settled down, so we rush back outside to sit around a bonfire or hike the trails. Nature more than meets us halfway, bursting into glorious color. Not one detail is left unperfected. If autumn means sitting on the porch in the fading light of sunset, drinking cider and watching my kids run around the brilliant auburn maple, I'll freeze time and stay here forever.

Gardens and growing things wind down, which means a break from constant work for growers and mowers. My freezer is stocked with tomato sauces, a harbinger of spaghetti dinners to come. Our shelves hold newly canned applesauce and jams waiting to be opened in a time of scarcity. Once again, I wonder what we'll do with all these pumpkins and squash piling up everywhere, fat and round and ripe.

Even city and suburban dwellers love harvesttime. We go a bit loony for our favorite traditions, piling into minivans, driving hours to let children pick pumpkins from massive fields and chase each other through cornstalk mazes. We fill our nostrils and bellies with apple-cider donuts and wrap our cold hands around hot cups of cider. We flock to apple orchards, where small children sample a bite from each piece of fruit before dropping it to the ground to choose another.

Harvest is gorgeous. It is the (exhausted) shout of victory, the reward after so much work. Whether our daily efforts are invested in fields, factories, or families, we live to build something to fruition. We take deep satisfaction in a project envisioned, brought to life, and completed.

Fields and forests burst into gold medals and red streamers: everything, everything shouts for joy. Remember all we vulnerably brought forward with hope? Remember how faithfully we worked, how hard we tried? We courageously stuck by our dreams, our efforts, haunted by the knowledge that there are no guarantees, that all our earnest faith might result in only loss and brokenness. But now, thanks be to God, we are here. A dream fulfilled lies finally in our hands, inviting us to taste and see. Can you savor it—the joy of liberation, the banishment of fears, the pleasures of rest, the sweetness of relief? *Oh, taste and see.*

Harvest overflows with relief and gratitude.

Thanksgiving Feasts

My family shops regularly at Costco, which conveniently provides seasonal items like strawberries, tomatoes, and asparagus in the same brightly colored packages year-round. But since time began, most humans ate in winter if, and only if, the harvest was plentiful enough to stockpile bounty for themselves and their livestock. If the harvest failed, famine could mean death while a community held out until the next year. That's more than enough time to lose everything you love. With this threat always in mind, people watched the skies, the air, the ground, counting the days until harvest. Then—when the fruit of so much work, sweat, planning, patience, and faithfulness was safely gathered and stored—the celebration began.

Can you feel the relief of the women and men, of the elderly and the children? *Together, we gave all we had, and it was enough. Raise a song of joy: We will survive another year.*

In cultures all around the world, successful harvest is celebrated with gratitude: festivals and feasts, music, singing, and dancing. Dishes of food weigh down tables. Prayers and hymns are offered, families are gathered, thanksgiving is lifted.

Each year, my family celebrates this annual feast by meeting my husband's tribe in a "cabin" in the mountains. (Once upon a time it *was* a cabin, but our numbers have swollen to thirty people, and I'd say "mansion" or "dormitory" would be a better word now.) Though none of us rely on our work in the fields to survive the winter months, we eagerly load the tables with squash and potatoes, greens and cranberries, turkey and stuffing and pie. When we cannot hold another bite, we go around the circle, each of us sharing an item of thanksgiving. We have survived another year, together, with God's help, and we are grateful for the tangible harvest we see in each other's lives. Some of us endured painful relationships and found healing. Some were unemployed but found work. Some had insurmountable needs, but we pulled together and discovered there was enough. We made it through with the help of each other, and we are still here, still together, still grateful.

Whatever the work we do, whatever the harvest, we need this chance to look back and remember the hope, the effort—and rejoice with thanksgiving. The baby, squealing as he takes his first steps. The graduate, throwing her hat into the air, clutching a hard-earned diploma. The relief of holding a child newly born or adopted, the sweet miracle after years of longing. The promotion, so long earned, that will finally provide enough for secure shelter, food, and healthcare. The man whose family can finally throw a long-awaited retirement party.

Gather together the family and friends, and kill the fatted calf! This is the season to rejoice.

Pirates and Parables

A teacher has come to town and, to no one's surprise, a crowd forms. This crowd has gathered steam for months, following him from village to village. Some listen out of curiosity, others with a passion to learn and grow. Still others are all-in, not just listening but following him, traveling the countryside as he goes from place to place.

Today, the crush of people makes speaking (not to mention listening) impossible. This throng is hardly controlled chaos. So the teacher climbs the side of a mountain and sits where his voice will carry to the people clustered below. To this community of farmers and fishermen, he talks about cultivation and harvest, the investments and rewards of their lives.

Blessed are the poor in spirit, he says, for they will receive the Kingdom. Those who mourn will receive comfort. Those who plant mercy will reap mercy. Those who are insulted and persecuted can rejoice, for their reward is in heaven. Those who do good to their enemies will receive a return from the Lord. Giving generously will result in more generosity; forgiveness will lead to forgiveness. Similarly, judgment will lead to more judgment, and worry to more worry. If you plant worry and greed, worry and money will be your only rewards. But if you seek for God's Kingdom and for righteousness, these greater things will be given to you.[1]

Jesus' words are meant to ring in the air, in the ears and hearts of the crowd milling about and the crowds that still listen for his words today. They echo through history, allowing us to meditate on them and be changed, bit by bit. What do we want our lives, our families, our world, to be? Are we investing, planting, nurturing goodness, shalom—or selfishness and greed? Are we cultivating the seeds we want to harvest?

The Kingdom of God, Jesus said, is like grain scattered, growing, then harvested. Like a mustard seed, impossibly small, yet becoming the largest plant of all. He tells of good soil, producing fruit and life—and of worthless soil, producing no harvest at all.[2]

James, the brother of Jesus, continued these themes

in the letter he wrote to the early believers. He points to the work and endurance required for harvest, considering the farmer who diligently puts seed into the ground, then waits for rain, patiently and faithfully caring for the "precious crop" until the time is right.[3] So, too, he says, we must strengthen our hearts as we wait for the harvest of Jesus' coming. He reminds us to plant seeds of peace in order to reap righteousness and the good fruits of wisdom, humility, praise, and goodness. Otherwise, we will plant and harvest envy, bitterness, selfishness, and evil. For, as Paul reminds us in his own letter, when God's Spirit lives in us, we harvest his life-giving fruit.[4]

Our spirits, our families, our communities—these are fertile soil, and they will grow *something*. It matters what we plant, what we water, what we tend. If we do not give up, Jesus and his disciples remind us again and again, we will reap a harvest. And what joyous celebration there is when our long, hard labor through storms and weeds and loss yields a crop of righteousness, justice, and peace.

When my son was about three, we were putting coats on one morning when he hurled a toy through the air and hit me squarely in the back. Words were said, including but not limited to, "It's not okay to throw things at people."

"But I'm a pirate," was his reply, "and pirates throw stones at other people."

I asked him where he learned this suspicious fact. "At Pirates' Cove," he replied, referring to a preschool-oriented theme park nearby. We both paused, searching for a stone-throwing memory from the Cove. "Well," he clarified, "it was in my *imagination* at Pirates' Cove."

"Okay, but even if you were a pirate, it would be mean to throw stones at people," I insisted.

A few minutes later, I was buckling him into his car seat. "I'm afraid of pirates," he announced, "because they might throw stones at me." I assured my son that there weren't many pirates around these days, and those who remained kept to the high seas. The chances of running into a stone-throwing pirate in our landlocked location were slim.

"You know," I pointed out as I started the car, "you probably won't ever meet a pirate, but you *will* occasionally meet someone who is being mean. Even then, it's nearly always best not to be mean back."

"Why?" he asked.

"Because then that person is mean, then you are mean back, then he is mean back, then you are mean back, then him, then you, then him, then you . . . and that's *so much* meanness!"

"And," I tagged on, "less meanness is better."

I decided to stick to the basics of ancient wisdom and save self-defense and alerting the authorities for another day.

My philosopher-son nodded sagely in the back seat.

Much later in the day, we were driving home again, having left our conversation about stone-throwing pirates far behind us. From his car seat, my preschooler piped up, "When we were at the beach, my friend Ian was playing with my watering can. When it was time to go, I took it away from him."

"Hmmm," I mused. "Did you take it from him in a nice way, or in a mean way?"

"In a mean way. And then Ian said 'No, that's mine! No! Mine!' and pulled it back. And that was mean too."

Then he sighed as only a sweet, mischievous preschooler can. With wisdom beyond his years he confessed, "I guess we were being pirates."

Right there in the car, a small taste of spiritual harvest: character sprouting and growing within my son and family.

What we grow in life is not limited to the work we do with our hands, in the garden or the office or the kitchen. Our spirits, our character—and those around us, too—are being formed each day, nurtured and cultivated by what we water and tend, what we choose, where we invest.

I give thanks for every glimpse of harvest.

The Close of Autumn

The first-frost smells of slightly frozen autumn are transcendent. Last night's temperatures brought all but the hardiest of this year's bounty to an end; yet when the first rays of early morning sun warm this frozen world, the result is a feast for all my senses. The fresh chill in the air exhilarates me as I draw it deep into my lungs. A carpet of frozen leaves crunches beneath my feet, releasing the sweet fragrance of decay. It is magical, this first frost.

Welcome to the close of autumn.

I sit with him this morning, the creator of all this, breathing it in. We sit on my front porch, drinking tea, listening to the unmistakable sound of gentle wind rustling through dried leaves, breathing in their sweet, tangy smells. I share with him my thoughts on fall: the joys of cooler temperatures, the beauty of autumn, the celebration of harvest. But also, my dislike of endings, my struggle against the inevitable coming of cold, dark days. I confess my preference for all that is green and growing, hopeful and alive.

He listens patiently, then reminds me of his side of the story. The creator of autumn is enthralled by the harvest of his handiwork. The blue-gray skies, raindrops that spontaneously appear in the air, the surplus of gourds, pumpkins, and burnt-orange mums. The warmth of sweaters, the comfort of sipping hot tea. The smell of decaying leaves—which I myself just described as transcendent. The brilliant colors of life in this harvest season. The gratitude of abundance, of fulfillment, of enough.

In nature, nothing is wasted. Fruits and vegetables may be harvested to provide life for another creature, but even if left to rot on the vine or in the field, they will fall and feed the soil, the worms and fungus recycling them back into the ground, readying them to spring forth into new life. Nothing is ever wasted or destroyed: only transformed.[5]

If this is the way God acts through creation, mightn't we expect him to work this way in our spirits as well? All our efforts, disappointments, victories, and failures—in his Kingdom, nothing is wasted. He is taking it all, shaping it, forming us, steadfastly working toward his own harvest festival in a world made new. Our Gardener can cultivate gratitude in me, even—perhaps especially—in the seasons I try to push away. For it is when I need him most that I remember to seek him . . . and find him.

Is this why he exhorts us to rejoice "in all circumstances"?[6] We walk boldly toward the close, choosing gratitude, believing that God's ultimate harvest will be justice, wholeness, redemption, shalom.

I sit quietly, taking it all in—the sights, smells, tastes, feelings, and sounds. I know he is making something new, even in this season of harvest, this close of autumn.

Because he is always, always making things new.

CULTIVATING GRATITUDE

The author of Ecclesiastes (and much later, Pete Seeger) reminds us that there is a time for everything: to be born and to die, to rejoice and to mourn, to plant and to harvest.[7] What aspects of your life are cycling toward closure these days? Where do you have an opportunity to express relief and gratitude? How has God met you in the fruit of your hopes and labors?

- Take a moment to **touch and feel** the rewards and harvests present in your life right now, whether it is a diploma, a trophy, a well-cooked dinner, a juicy blueberry, or a person you're investing in. Embrace the fruit of a job well done (or at least, well begun).

- As you allow this "harvest" to be physically present with you, **rejoice in the goodness** of completion and contentment. Speak out your gratitude to God . . . or sing it!

- Lift your arms, or face, or heart in **worship and surrender** to the God who was, and is, and is to come—who is never-ending. Whatever your harvest is in this season, rest in the light of his presence shining on your face.

CHAPTER 8

LEAVES

Surrender

Autumn has caught us in our summer wear.

PHILIP LARKIN, *COLLECTED POEMS*

When my heart draws close
To the close of autumn
Your love abounds.

"CLOSE OF AUTUMN," CAEDMON'S CALL

DURING BREAKFAST this morning, my family noticed something happening in the yard. Shadows floated past the blinds. We could hear soft movement on the ground. As I opened the curtains to investigate, my son ran outside to conduct a more thorough investigation.

In a flash, he was back inside, slamming the door, yelling for us all to come outside. "You have to see this! You have to!"

And so we did, pulling on sweatshirts and slipping on shoes as we went. Down the stairs and into the yard, right to the enormous walnut tree outside our kitchen window.

As recently as an hour ago, it had retained all but a handful of its thousands of leaves. But now, this morning, it was entirely bare. All at once, it had let go, releasing each and every leaf, sending them floating to the ground. We stood there, our feet sinking into the thick carpet of freshly fallen leaves, golden confetti falling all around us as though we had stepped into an autumn snow globe.

I don't know why this majestic walnut decided to hold on for so long, then let go all at once. But I do know how and why it lets go eventually. The green leaves, grown each spring, serve the trees by catching sunlight, turning the warm rays of energy into food and nourishment for the entire organism. But in autumn, the days grow too short, and the light too scarce. Soon, the cold freezes the leaves, killing them—if they stay, there will be no room for new life to begin in the spring, to catch the sun and create much-needed food. Without letting go now of what has been lovely and helpful and good, there can be no "next."

And so, thousands and thousands of gorgeous maples, ashes, and oaks—flaming red and orange and auburn—allow the future to flow from the present. To live next year, they must not grasp hold of life but release.

The five of us tilt our faces to this shower of leaves, our pink noses absorbing the sweet, cold scent of frost and decay, flecks of gold and red tangling in our hair. And above it all, the strong, tall branches of this old, old tree, now entirely brown and bare.

The time had come to let go.

Of Trees and Wheat

On this earth, with its ebbs and flows of life and death, it is paramount we learn the bittersweet art of release. For paradoxically, when we grasp, we do not gain as we intend. Instead, we lose the perspective and grace to see the life to come, born from the endings of now; we lose the strength and mastery to wrest something lasting from what is fleeting. But how? How do we allow God to cultivate in us a heart of surrender?

Trees have been a long-standing icon for this faithful journey of letting go. Is it because they tower over us with so much dignity and grace, majestically releasing their leaves when the time comes? Perhaps it is their deep-rootedness and their age, and we acknowledge them as elders. Perhaps it is because we watch this cycle from beginning to end, year after year. We observe how fresh beginnings culminate in vibrancy, then come to an end—and hide the seeds of tomorrow as they go.

Ever since the tree of knowledge in the Garden, we have considered trees our teachers and mentors. The opening words of the book of Psalms describe a wise and righteous person who, like a tree, is planted by the river, yielding fruit in season.[1] We imagine a thriving tree heavy-laden with nearly harvestable fruit; but to bear fruit *in season*, the tree must weather a time *out of season.*

If we accept the years that burst forth with life and joy, we must also accept those that ask us to relinquish the life we hold. To everything, there is a season. While we tend to fight and scream when the time comes, nature vividly, expertly demonstrates how to release with utmost beauty, power, and grace.

Jesus, the Son of God, did not grasp or clutch at power and life as I'm so prone to do. He let go, emptied himself. Releasing status and glory, he became human, was born, lived life not as a king but as a peasant under oppressive imperialist rule. He went on emptying himself even of that body and life, demonstrating what his farming friends already knew: Unless a grain of wheat falls to the ground, it remains only a single seed. But if it falls, and dies, it produces abundant seeds, abundant life.[2] Jesus, God-made-flesh, emptied himself, allowed himself to fall and die and become the firstfruits of new life.

Are we ready to practice and master this lesson? Surrender is a valley that life demands we walk through, ready or not. We will fare much better if we are prepared.

Like Jesus' first students, we don't need to take his word for it. Each and every one of us has watched the trees empty their beauty into the wind. Grasses and plants, long since dried and brittle, burst open to allow their seeds to fall into the cold breeze. The pumpkins I turned into jack-o'-lanterns (then left on my front porch for far too long) split open in their decay, spilling seeds of new life onto the ground.

How exactly like life this is. Subtly, stealthily moving forward for the win right at the very moment of defeat and death. This sounds just like our Creator, a classic strategy of the one who made this world with its cycles and circles, who came and let his own body be split, opening forth through death the pathway to eternal life. By his creative decree, the actual biological process of decay is not, as it seems, sinister but hopeful. The earth invites life to pour forth from death.

Our futures pour from God's hands in the same way, if we can find the strength to receive them. After a lifetime on this earth, we know exactly what is coming. There is no excuse for being surprised.

In theology, the word for Jesus' example is *kenosis*: emptying.[3] Kenosis refers to the Incarnation, but also to God's character and inclination, his ethic, his signature move. He is a God who empties himself, sacrificing himself so that creation might thrive and come to life. He asks this also of us, his children. We, too, must empty ourselves, not clutching, but releasing.

We let go of what has been, with an eye on what is to come. Mastering this lesson takes a lifetime of practice. Embedded within are so many additional lessons—humility, surrender, courage, contentment, acceptance, and above all, wisdom. As the Serenity Prayer reminds us, there are things we cannot change and things we *must* change. We need wisdom to know the difference.[4]

Born to Trouble

When I was growing up, it was stylish to declare a life verse, as one might declare a major at school. We slipped this verse into casual conversations, résumés, or testimonies like a personal brand. The Bible contains 31,102 verses, so mathematically, the odds are high that most people would have a unique life verse. What are the chances you would overlap with someone else in your Bible study with so many to choose from?

But of course, some verses make better slogans than others. No one is likely to choose a snippet of genealogy, or a war-and-famine-and-pestilence tag line. Frankly, most of the narratives don't break down into pithy quotes well at all. So most life verses end up something like: *I can do all things through Christ who strengthens me* or *Trust in the LORD with all your heart . . . and he will make straight your paths.* Or the ever-popular *For I know the plans I have for you . . . plans to prosper you and not to harm you, plans to give you hope and a future.*[5]

It's understandable that we want to reduce faith into the wind beneath our wings, the Lord a lucky talisman in our pocket. But I worry about discipleship in a faith community drenched in these promises without the rest of the text. A focus on such verses (out of context) risks making our faith into just that—a good-luck charm to carry around.

Then what happens when things fall apart? In truth, during some seasons, we stumble through pain and confusion, as everything we thought we knew about life appears false, and despair seems closer than hope. Too many of us walk away from God and faith when we discover that life includes pain and suffering, that the arc of our life stories both ebbs and flows, that sometimes we must open our hands and let go. We haven't practiced the wisdom that comes from surrender, the strength that comes from following the cycles of life and death all the way around. We have learned how to stand on the promises, but not to surrender to a God we can trust even in the darkness of loss. It seems too many of us believed we were promised a life of ease, with God parting the waters before us and no storms on the horizon.

I'm not a pessimist, but I find some of the most comforting verses in the Bible to be those like Job 5:7: "Yet man is born to trouble as surely as sparks fly upward."

Have you ever huddled around a bonfire on a cool evening, roasting marshmallows or enjoying friends? The folks who wrote (and listened to) the book of Job probably huddled before a fire every day, if not every meal. There was no central heating anywhere on the planet. Every day, they watched and *knew*: a fire gives off sparks, and the sparks fly upward. This is reality, plain and simple. There's nothing to discuss, no controversy, no reason to complain. These are the facts of life.

Another thing they observed just as clearly and simply: We are born to trouble.

The people we need and love the most die—often suddenly and tragically, anytime from conception to old age. Those we rely on let us down. Our bodies are prone to disease, sometimes debilitating ones that shorten or alter our lives. Injustice is thick and systemic, evil acts are perpetrated everywhere. Suffering—not just a bad cold or a disappointment, but the real thing—is part of life.

And yet, somehow many of us believe that utmost success and ease are due us, as our life verses seemed to promise. So when the reality of life hits, it feels as though God has done something wrong. We're clutching these hopeful Bible verses and browsing page after page of our friends' bright and cheerful social-media posts, but we've never considered the context of any of them. God's faithfulness to Israel takes place over thousands of years of slavery, exile, and oppression. That requires a long, long surrender before the promise. God's redemption of creation is still pending completion, though the wait has been unfathomably prolonged.

Our friends' smiling Facebook photos freeze one beautiful, cheery moment out of a thousand, rarely including the tantrums, fighting, and trips to the toilet taking place that same day. We've tricked ourselves into expecting that life is or should be a fairy tale, that we can *and we will* live happily ever after. But no. Real life comes to us unabridged, a complete package of beauty and joy, transcendence and ecstasy—and grief and trouble, pain and confusion.

As the sparks fly upward.

God cultivates in us the skills of hope, of perseverance, of rejoicing—but also of surrender. Not one true story in history has ever depicted or suggested life free of grief and struggle, and neither does the Bible. If anything, the Bible highlights the troubles of life too vividly for most of us to stomach. That's why we skip over the brutal scenes and move quickly to the hopeful declarations of redemption.

Jesus *promises* that in this world we will have trouble.[6] Not promises like a gift but promises like certainty. *This is life*. We can count on it. You can take it to the bank.

The idea that we could or should live happily ever after stems from our stories of privilege, not from God's promises. Hope isn't the American dream. Hope knows that we are born to trouble *and* that God is here. That he is both transcendent and immanent, Creator and Redeemer. That he has overcome. Hope invites us to look endings square in the face and surrender, letting go of what was good and alive to receive what will come—whatever will come—from God's hand.

Science demonstrates what faith traditions have always taught: Pushing negative feelings away or fighting against them only empowers them, increasing our suffering and limiting our power to overcome. Paradoxically, by accepting these seasons of struggle and loss and the impact they have on our minds and bodies, we gain mastery and freedom. In accepting the reality of death and pain, we gain life and peace.

And these fantasies of perfect lives, fulfilling vocations, beautiful marriages and children we've clutched so tightly? God invites us to stand courageously facing the future, acknowledging the truth—then open our hands and hearts and dreams to him . . . and release.

Friend, God is still here. Every step of the way, whether you go willingly or kicking and screaming, he is with you—and he has gone before you. Will you reach out your hands and find that he is still right here?

Completion

The surprise twist of autumn, of our jobs well-done and now complete, is the startling reality of that last word: *complete.*

For the past eight months, I've gone out to my garden every day. I loved being surrounded by all this life-giving life. I even tried to embrace the hordes of mud and bugs that inevitably hitch a ride into the house on the stems and leaves and roots. As summer wound down into autumn, the bounty began to taper off. Instead of a kitchen full of over-ripe produce and fruit flies, I scoured the garden for anything still producing—an occasional bunch of kale or one final green tomato.

But then November rolled around, and with it, a hard freeze.

I knew it was coming, and I knew what it meant. Still, the next morning, I found myself asking, "I wonder if I can find enough flowers to make a bouquet?" and "What could I grab from the garden to make for lunch?" Old habits die harder than vegetables, I guess. I meandered outside and was taken aback: every single plant withered and entirely dead. Their forms, just yesterday alive, now skeletal and frozen.

There was no life left at all.

I wasn't born yesterday, and this isn't my first autumn. I know exactly what the terms are in life, yet they still take me by surprise, still knock the wind out of me. I stood among my raised beds gasping at death where so recently we celebrated abundant life. We are here for a season, which gives birth to the next and then fades away. A season was never meant to be more than it is—and neither are we. We must learn to let go.

But God wasn't born yesterday either, and this hasn't been his first season of endings. The good news, proclaimed by all creation since that first story in the Garden, is that this is *God's* story, and he is determined to bring his creation to redemption, to shalom. Christians have always declared that after Christ let go of life, he descended into the grave, unlocked the shackles of death, and rose victorious in resurrection—not primarily for himself, but as the firstfruits of a redeemed creation.

CULTIVATING SURRENDER

In some seasons of life, we seem to have no choice but to let go of everything at once. What do you need to release in your life now? Once you have let these things go, what will endure? What will remain? Where is God present in this letting go, and how can you awaken to him?

- **Make a list, draw a picture, or write a poem** about the things in your life that you need to surrender. Allow these things to live and be loved, to be acknowledged for their value in your life.
- **Breathe deeply** and practice remaining present *in this moment* with God and these things you have identified. Know that right now, he is here with you.

- Find a tangible way to **lift these things to the Lord and let go**. Surrender them with gratitude for what has been and hope for what will be.
- **Receive from the Lord** the future that is to come. He is already there.

CHAPTER 9

TWILIGHT

Trust

Abide with us, O Lord, for it is toward the evening and the day is far spent . . . Abide with us in the evening of the day, in the evening of life, in the evening of the world.

ANONYMOUS[1]

It's a long, long while from May to December,
But the days grow short when you reach September.

MAXWELL ANDERSON, "SEPTEMBER SONG"

THE SUN IS GONE for the day, sunk low beneath the horizon line. But light lingers on. Walking home, I'm wonderstruck by the sky as it performs a thousand marvels all at once. Palettes of color drape across the firmament, seamlessly moving from one hue to the next: from the fiery blaze at the horizon to the deep-midnight blue at the dome's apex, speckled with the first stars of evening. There's a chill in the air, and the sound of a million living things coming awake now, here at the end. Insects and animals who thrive in these moments of half-light send a rustling song to usher out the day and greet the night. As the saturation of color fades to gray, other senses awaken to the thrill of crickets, the softness of stillness, the peace of transition poised between one thing and the next.

This is the fleeting, magical moment of twilight; light and dark, night and day delicately balanced, like the last sustained notes of a concerto reverberating before the magnificent silence at the close.

If you blink, you will miss it.

Autumn, too, is a twilight, a mystical, magical, time-between-times. The equilibrium between life and death, the balance between what was and what will be. By day, the fading autumn light is gorgeous. Golden rays shine down slantingly, setting everything aglimmer, reflecting off the showers of leaves raining down like confetti, like playful applause. But by afternoon, the brilliant, blazing sunset announces twilight far too early. Dusk takes the stage in midafternoon when everyone is around to watch the magic. Long before bedtime we're blanketed in darkness.

Yesterday when my kids and I arrived home from school pickup, the sun was nearly set. A few hours later, when my husband joined us around the supper table, the world had plunged into deep darkness. I asked my children if these dim afternoons felt cozy or depressing. "Cozy!" one announced. "Depressing," moaned another. "Cozy *and* depressing," mused the third, always the peacemaker.

This space is neither day nor night, neither the heat of summer nor the cold of winter. And so, we begin a new tradition. Stepping outside, we watch the sunset splashing color across the western horizon. We search the blackening sky for bodies of twinkling light, soaking in every moment of magic. Back in the house we play the song "Close of the Day"[2] and go from room to room, closing curtains and blinds. Then we gather in the kitchen and light one symbolic candle, remembering that God's light shines even as our earthly lights fade. Remembering that we have no reason to fear.

Betwixt and Between

Twilight has historically been considered religiously auspicious, for the same reasons poets, painters, and photographers favor it: an ethereal, otherworldly beauty falls across the land and sky. God seekers have always taken note of this hour. Ancient religions held rituals at twilight. Early Christians held evening prayers and annual vigils during these moments poised in the balance.

The ancient Celts in particular saw spiritual value in this time-between-times. For them, the world was separated into two opposites: light and dark. Each twenty-four-hour period was divided into day and night, with twilight forming the doorway between. Each year, too, was split between dark months and light months, with spring and autumn providing the sacred bridge. These thresholds were times-between-times, betwixt and between. Neither one thing nor another, these ambiguous moments brimmed over with creative spiritual possibility. As a result, anything symbolizing transition was considered consecrated: doorways, intersections, thresholds, bridges, the place and time of births and deaths.

The ancient Celts passed these traditions on to the Celtic Christians who came after them, and the places and times betwixt and between became doorways to God himself, pregnant with opportunity to be awash in God's presence. Transitions like twilight or autumn were considered holy places where heaven and earth might collide, where the overlay of Creator and creation grew permeable so the holy and mundane could meet and mingle, where his Spirit might fall on mortals like us.

Is there truly something sacred in these intersections between time and place? I believe that we can meet and mingle with God in any moment, for he is here, always. But I love the notion that these occasions of crossing-over can act as sacramental reminders, holy invitations to encounter him, to learn from him.

Of course, not everything considered powerful and holy is approachable. More than a tinge of fear mixed into the Celts' understanding of these doorways—which doesn't surprise me at all. Stepping into the unknown can be frightening. Walking forward into darkness is not for the faint of heart.

But we know the one who awaits us on the other side.

The fading light is lovely, full of colors and sounds we could not see or hear before. God is present, teaching us to trust by offering himself. He is not anxious about what lies ahead, for he is there too, on the other side of the door, in that other-place-that-is-not-this-place. After all, where can we go from his presence?

In the peace of autumn's twilight, God walks beside us as we head toward the night.

Tabernacles

The families of Israel awaken outside again, in hastily built shelters just as their ancestors did hundreds of years ago, a thousand years and more. But today, they do not face dubious survival in the wilderness. Today, they are celebrating the weeklong autumn festival of *Sukkot* or *Feast of Tabernacles.* Each family sleeps in their *sukkah*, which symbolizes both the tents erected in the fields and orchards for laborers to sleep in during the busy season of harvest and a reminder that God brought his people out of slavery in Egypt to live in tents in the desert.

In both cases, the bottom line is the same: Our Creator has provided through every generation—and he will again. During the lean times of history, and the lean times we face in the winter ahead, we rely on his provision to see us through.

These are holy days, seven days of celebration, ceremony, and services. Each family—surrounded by neighbors and throngs of visiting strangers—have sung hosannas and psalms, recited blessings, heard the Torah, shared meals.

You are a shelter, Lord, to every generation.

Here, in the space between one day's end and the next day's beginning, a sacred ritual of light is performed each evening of the festival. The temple priests burn towering menorahs, symbolizing the fading light, imploring God to bring them through the darkening season and return the sunshine in spring. Music and torch dances continue all through the night—a spectacular memorial of reliance on God to bring the light, to *be* the light.

It is here that the man named Jesus stands up. Interrupting this ancient, holy ritual, he proclaims to the crowd in a loud voice, "*I am the light of the world.* Whoever follows me will never walk in darkness, but will have the light of life."[3]

Who is this man? The community gathered in this time-between-times—this autumn, this evening—to acknowledge that all we have received, all which keeps us alive, comes from the Creator. Then this man insists it comes from *him*.

What must it have been like, hearing Jesus that day? As the community gathered for seven days of festivals, celebrating their certainty that our faithful God would steadfastly provide as the sun faded into darkness, Jesus announced that the provision was already granted, that God was present, in him.

No wonder some followed him. No wonder most tried to silence him. A man in their midst, a neighbor, one of them, prone to illness and aging and exhaustion as we all are, associating himself with the ancient cycles of light and darkness. Claiming that *he* was the gift of salvation, inserting himself as the sacred provision for which they implored the one and only God.

Around the world, we still celebrate the fading light in a thousand different ways, a hundred different festivals marking this time-between-times, this hinge between warmth and cold, between the death of the sun and our hope for its rebirth. Today in my house, during the last days of autumn, we string lights on an evergreen tree and burn Advent candles, proclaiming with all the stubbornness of hope that the Messiah has come and made his tabernacle, his tent, his *sukkot* in our midst, and remains here still. We insist that this twilight is a bridge to something new, that God stands on both sides of this doorway and offers us *himself.*

Then and now, our Creator reminds us daily that we can enter the future without fear, for he is there. There is no future, no darkness, where he is not already present. We may step forward boldly, with certainty.

We believe that the true light that gives life to all people has come into the world.

The Afternoon of Life

An aging woman sits on the ancient tree stump outside her home. Her old eyes can see little in the dim light of dusk, and in the late afternoon of her life, she lacks the strength for hard physical work. So instead, as younger adults prepare the evening meal, she sits and tells stories to the children who assemble in the gathering darkness, stories of her life and the lessons learned through failure and success, gains and losses. Wisdom travels from her age to their youth as they meet in the balance between day and night, between her generation and theirs—gifts they will need to anchor them on this journey. Her knowledge will allow these young ones to recognize the pathway without having seen it themselves. She is the keeper of memories, the guardian of tradition, the steady candle that lights the way into their youthful unknown.

She, too, is facing the unknowable future, and not with

the energy or hope that the children rolling and bouncing at her feet carry effortlessly. But she has something else: In her age, now in the afternoon of her life, she has been around the sun many times. She knows that to everything, there is a season, that joys are fleeting, but trouble will not overtake or overcome. She has learned to travel in peace, without fear.

Youth observes twilight years with disbelief. Whether they hold the aging in esteem or contempt, it seems inconceivable that they themselves will reach such a place. But the journey of years will accumulate quickly, and they will arrive here all the same. The creative, courageous energy of youth, so quickly engulfed by the exhausting, fulfilling abundance of work, finally slows down with the passage of time. When we finally reach the afternoon of life, we have earned the right to rest, to pass on to others what we have learned by surviving so many ups and downs, and to share the trust we formed along the way. Less strength for physical labor provides more time to ponder years of experience, lessons, and wisdom. As the light dims, we sort through piles of memories to find the meaning we missed in the chaos—and gift it to others, a light to illuminate their way.

It was Carl Jung who described the decades during and after middle age as the afternoon of life. Jung believed that our developmental task in these years is to deepen our sense of meaning, an opportunity to move from a rushed first draft to a final masterpiece. Our declining outward strength is not designed to limit our contribution to society but to allow for *internal* work: maturity, understanding, perspective. In the wake of the body's slower pace, the spirit can thrive, providing us with something profoundly important to share, a voice of assurance our community dearly needs. We can face the unknown doorways when our loved ones have shown us the way. Jung says,

> The afternoon of life is just as full of meaning as the morning; only, its meaning and purpose are different.[4]

He expounds on this idea:

> The significance of the morning undoubtedly lies in the development of the individual, our entrenchment in the outer world, the propagation of our kind, and the care of our children. This is the obvious purpose of nature. . . .
>
> In primitive tribes we observe that the old people are almost always the guardians of the mysteries and the laws . . . How does the matter stand with us? Where is the wisdom of our old people, where are their precious secrets and their visions?[5]

My husband's grandmother was an artist in the afternoon of her own life. She spent hours wandering the beach outside her home, sorting through the sand, debris, and seaweed, looking for something beautiful worth saving. One of her favorite items to collect was sea glass.

Sea glass refers to beautiful pieces of frosty-colored glass that have been worn down by decades of tumbling around the salty waters and rough beaches of the ocean. Real sea glass takes up to one hundred years to form, a thing of beauty emerging out of a lifetime of ebbs and flows. These treasures symbolize the magic of autumn and of twilight, for only after years of hard refining does the beauty emerge.

The pounding ocean waves and tides are constant in their changes. They rise, then fall—as do the floodwaters of the river valleys, the heat of the seasons, the daily light of the sun. Only after a lifetime of rolling through the ebbs and flows do we gather a glimpse of the beauty created in the balance, the sea glass, the wisdom.

It takes close to one hundred years for a human life to form to completion as well. Can we enter the afternoon of life in peace, fortified with enough trust to recognize that our Creator will be true through the changes and present with us to the end? Our loved ones are standing just on the other side of the threshold, holding out a candle for us, encouraging us to keep our heads held high. Our young ones are behind us, watching closely as we light their path and teach them how and whom to trust.

Humanity has always relied on the gentle shepherding of older generations—those who, like sand, like sea glass, have weathered a lifetime of cycles and changes, who have been worn by the crashes of life into something true. Those approaching twilight have learned from the sifting and the sorting where God's Spirit resides and what he says to us all—and how to sit quietly enough to listen and receive.

The song of life is as brilliant as ever, here in the moments before darkness. Can you hear it? Can you feel it? Autumn's song is not a requiem but an anthem of joy, of gratitude, for all that passes but still lingers in this moment—and a certainty that *he* will walk beside us through every doorway, that he already waits on the other side.

Tonight, my family lingers at our favorite local haunt: a living-history farm that freezes time from the 1890s. We've "helped" with chores and meandered through meadows, gardens, and trees. Now, finally, in the chill of autumn twilight, we head toward home.

We're soon overtaken on the dirt path by two farmers who are leading several horses out to pasture for the evening. Stepping aside, we watch as four magnificently strong animals march by, stepping up to the gates: the threshold between the day's work and the evening's rest. Time seems to pause for a moment, suspended in the time-between-times.

Then, with a pat on their rumps, the horses are set free. They break into a gallop, into the golden light of evening, through the golden fields of autumn. We stand, transfixed, watching, until they disappear beyond the ridge.

This day, this year, is over, and there's no turning back the clock. In this twilight, at this crossroads, we stand at the intersection of one thing ending, another thing not yet begun. There is mystery here, and God's presence, if we can find the courage to walk forward in him, trusting he will be there in the dark: the Light of the World.

CULTIVATING TRUST

What is your first reaction to transitions, to the threshold between one thing and another? The adventure may beckon us to stay engaged, but our fears for the future may hold us back. Where is God to be found in these time-between-times?

- When you see the sun setting on another day, **remember that Jesus is the light of the world**, that God's salvation is here in our midst. Allow these natural ceremonies of light—twilight, dawn, autumn's darkness, summer's brightness, the shining sun, moon, and stars—to remind you that he is here, present with us.
- Set aside time—an hour, a day, or a weekend—and **intentionally reflect** on the ebbs and flows you have survived. Consider all you have learned in the process, the trust gained through prior victory.
- **Record the lessons** you've accumulated over the years in a journal, a painting, or a song—whatever is a natural expression for you. Look for authentic ways to pass along to others these lessons God has granted you.
- **Look at the physical doorways**, thresholds, and intersections in your life. Leave a Post-it or a picture to remind you that God walks with you through every change, that he is already waiting on the other side.

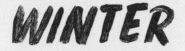

WINTER

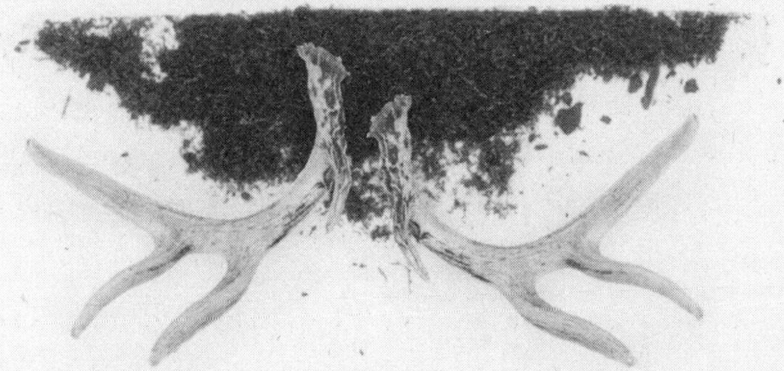

1.

the season between autumn and spring

2.

the coldest season of the year

3.

a period of inactivity or decay[1]

CHAPTER 10

SNOW

Rest

So long as you haven't experienced
this: to die, and so to grow,
you are only a troubled guest
on the dark earth.

GOETHE, "THE HOLY LONGING"

Fulfill now, O Lord, our desires and petitions
as may be best for us.

A PRAYER OF ST. CHRYSOSTOM, *THE BOOK OF COMMON PRAYER*

I WAKE IN THE MIDDLE of the night to an awareness that something is different, softer. I can't put a name to it, but there is a powerful and peaceful presence surrounding me. The world is moving almost imperceptibly, sound without noise.

Lying still for a moment, I take it in—the feeling of being rocked gently.

As consciousness overtakes me, I realize what is tickling the outer edges of my perception. I get out of bed and walk across the room. Softy lifting the blinds, I peek outside and see it: a billion diamonds falling slowly from the sky.

They have piled up into satin mounds, knee-high, waist-deep, covering everything. Piles and piles of pure white shimmer from the ground, the trees, the rooftops, the streetlights. Grass, sidewalk, and roads are indistinguishable. The whole wide world has been covered with a blanket and invited into deep, life-giving sleep.

Snow discreetly covers death and decay with loveliness and peace, like a gentle hand closing the eyes, like a shroud lovingly drawn across the body, like flower petals dusted on a new grave.

Snow declares "closed for construction" and "pardon our dust"—for the earth is indeed closed for now. So much has been put behind us, forever. But this sleep is not the dreadful despair it appears to be. Underneath, out of sight, a brand-new world is being constructed out of the old. Snow is the promise of something wonderful still to come.

For now, we say good-bye and move indoors, while the world rests.

Cabin Fever

Of course, what began as midnight magic transforms into morning mayhem. Even if we unbury the car, there's a layer of ice underneath the snow. There's no use scraping the windshield when the locks are frozen shut. Also, the roads are blocked by a foot of accumulation, so we're stuck until the plows come by to rescue us. School is closed, plans are cancelled, and *someone* must shovel the sidewalk.

The enchantment of being snowbound is romantic for a while, but our schedules don't easily accommodate being stuck at home. Responsibilities continue as always, productivity hardly skips a beat. Bosses expect us at work, and—thanks to electricity, automobiles, Internet, and furnaces—no one intends to spend the winter months cooped up resting, huddled together. We aim to overcome dormancy entirely.

Yet it isn't just the wild plants and animals whose lives grind to a halt in winter. Between the cold, snow, ice, and influenza, we're trapped in our dens more often than we'd like. I grow discouraged when I'm entombed inside for weeks on end, when the only fresh air available burns my lungs with cold, when one by one, my entire family falls victim to yet another virus.

We can't move forward during dormant seasons, and we hate limitations, despise being told to sit down and wait. Long stretches of imposed rest seem unfertile, useless, meaningless. We may be hit by an hour or two of unexpected airport delay or have decades stolen by illness or crisis, but this is the plain truth: Life occasionally screeches to a standstill. We fight against this with all we have, mutinously straining to move forward anyway.

But the reality of creation is that new growth relies on the potential cultivated during fallow, dormant seasons. The busyness of abundant life had this in mind all along: Bodies were fattened, and larders stocked, to make space for rest. Nature prepared itself to survive. Another growing time will come soon; now, sleep.

All of nature is sleeping now. We can't imagine trees,

flowers, seeds, bugs, viruses, or bacteria tucked into bed, but they are. Insufficient daylight and frigid temperatures mean inadequate food and water. Nearly every living thing escapes into hibernation, pushed to the brink of what can be considered alive, conserving energy to survive. We bury perennial roots and bulbs under blankets of dried leaves, hoping they will endure. Grandpa's beloved roses, next year's garlic bulbs, and my husband's artichoke plants—we're taking a risk on them all. We won't know for months what makes it through.

Snowbound at home, I feel the same way, staring at the tree outside my window. I have seen it bursting with blossoms, with vibrant green, with autumnal flame. But today, this creature seems lifeless. Nowhere on its huge bulk is any sign of life—not the smallest leaf or flower or bud or squirrel or bird. If I had never seen winter before, I would conclude that this majestic tree was over, done with, entirely dead. This powerful plant, once so full of life, is dormant.

Dormancy may come just when we need it, or when we most fear it. We love vacations, spa days, even the occasional snow day. Sometimes, we're grasping at any opportunity to sit and rest. But at other times, our "no" is spoken for us without consultation or consent. We may spend months or years hibernating in a dormancy we didn't request, physically, emotionally, spiritually—or all three at once. Whether slowed by disease, depression, pregnancy, infertility, family needs, divorce, job loss, or unexpected loneliness, we see these seasons as wasted, meaningless. We chafe against the silence and lifelessness in panic, alienation, and loss. *What if it goes on too long? Who am I in this season? Where has my real, creative, joyful self gone?* These questions haunt us all when the bursts of excitement and ideas and productivity dry up, when our spirits become as lifeless as the branches of my maple tree.

Friend, if you find yourself in this place, take hope. This season of rest is a necessary stop on the circling pathway of life. Without these cycles of silence and stillness, nothing new can come forth. We breathe in, breathe out, and then rest. We wake and begin a day's work, then sleep. Spring, summer, autumn, and winter. Every conceivable sequence relies on these ebbs and flows, bursting out strong and then slowly winding down—all in preparation to begin again. Just as the snow blankets the gray, barren land with sleep, what appears to us as death is very much the opposite. This rest time is the key to life. In dormancy, we become spring-loaded with potential.

What should we do with these days? We can sit, wrapped cozy in slippers and blankets, to wait it out or bundle up, run outside, and learn how to snow ski. However we choose to spend our dormancy, life will bear her fruit at the proper time.

Sleep and Sabbath

I love sneaking into my children's bedrooms after they've fallen asleep. Seeing their slumbering bodies sprawled out among quilts and stuffed animals never ceases to amaze me.

These busy, rambunctious creatures go nonstop for fourteen hours a day and then—collapse. Entirely. It's as though someone flipped a switch and cut off the power, and they flopped down in midplay. Vulnerable, utterly defenseless, they lie still for hours and hours. Where are they? It seems to me their spirits have been abducted or slipped into the Matrix.

What is this marvel called sleep?

More bizarre still is the fact that I do this too. And so do you! We all sleep, each one of us, every single day. Dozing off is the most commonplace thing, really; it happens daily, to everyone.

Just as our breath ebbs and flows each moment, our energy ebbs and flows each day. Without sleep, we can't live. We foolishly claim, "I'll sleep when I'm dead" or brag about how much work we accomplish with so little rest. But the truth is that sleep isn't laziness, but investment. We simply cannot keep going without these strange hours of powering down to reboot.

By Hebrew calculation, these hours of sleep are not only necessary but primary. The Hebrew day begins at sundown. Activity winds down as the warmth and light of the sun gradually diminish, and a new day begins with rest. "And there was evening, and there was morning"[1] is how Genesis describes the flow of the first day. By the Creator's design, sleep is not what happens when we run out of energy, tacked on at the end if we must. Sleep is where we *begin*, lying vulnerable and unproductive in the hands of God, preparing our bodies to meet the demands that will come soon enough. In sleep, potential is born.

Then the Hebrew cycles of sleep and work culminate with an extended weekly rest: Sabbath. From sundown to sundown, no work can be done. Resting becomes a sacred act. Observing the liturgy of an intentional pause each week allows for refreshment and realignment, not only for ourselves but for everyone and everything. After all, our children, employees, animals, and land must rest too. We make room for creativity, for worship and reliance on God, for justice and shalom, and the renewal of all things. In choosing the practice of Sabbath, we realize just how much depends on our ability to let go and rest in him. In learning the value of intentional dormancy, we prepare ourselves to survive the forced seasons of waiting when they come.

I get the feeling that these cycles of work and rest are one of our Creator's pet inventions, that perhaps there's something immensely important he wants us to gain through this constant repetition. After all, he gave our bodies no choice but to continue practicing this reliance on rest, and even included the Sabbath among the Ten Commandments. Yet we are just as stubborn in our rebellion. Prohibitions against murder and adultery we can understand, but against working every seventh day? We dislike and distrust rest—and the limits to our sovereignty that rest implies—above all else. Which of the commandments do we gloss over and leave behind, if not the fourth? We'll leave potential behind if it requires us to sit still for a day.

And yet, on average, half of each day is lived in darkness. The sun goes down, and then what? Only darkness. Only waiting. We sleep, helplessly at the mercy of whatever may be out there, for hours at a time. We do all we can to avoid it, but God made this, too—and he is still here in the dark. Only he stays eternally awake, on vigil always.

Beautiful Silence

Tramping through the snow, I stop for a moment. Everything around me is perfectly still. Only my footprints break the surface of the pure, white snow, and even these are behind me and out of sight. As far as my eyes can see, the world is untouched, asleep. The slumbering trees are soundless, with no leaves to wave in the breeze. The air itself is cold and still, hanging like icicles as I breathe. No birds, bugs, or animals scurry past. Only the blanket of snow and the deep covering of silence surround me on all sides.

Silence is the force undergirding the potential of dormancy, yet we avoid quietness and all that rises in the stillness. With the nonstop hustle made possible by electricity, we have all but annihilated silence from our lives. I must only speak the word, and music—any music written anytime or anywhere—fills my house. Magically, I conjure the voice of any loved one, anywhere in the world, at no cost. By simply uttering a question, I connect to any information I can imagine, within seconds. And yet the downside of this bounty we carry in our back pockets is that we have lost our ability to plumb the rich depths of being still.

Silence—terrifying, illuminating, gorgeous silence—is a

gift from God. But we have buried her in our love of noise and commotion.

When we turn off the podcasts, playlists, twenty-four-hour news, reality shows, and social-media feeds, we're left with nothing shielding us from the two voices we most fear encountering: our own and God's. We're left naked, forced to examine what is left when our idols and false identities have been stripped away.

Yet, we need the discomfort of nakedness, lest the fortress of idols we build around ourselves overtake and consume us. Like going to the dentist or scheduling a physical, we must regularly, intentionally strip down all that shields us from silence and dormancy so it does not kill us first. As much as we may hate to admit it, there is life-giving potential in turning everything off for a bit.

Jan Johnson, a spiritual director, describes these unguarded times alone with ourselves and God as the riskiest and most vulnerable, for we are wide open before him. She describes how, in the silence, we discover all those things we don't want to see—our faults, shame, grief, and loss. We're required to surrender, to trust, to put our money where our mouth is—for, as Jan rightly acknowledges, in this moment of vulnerability "our theology about God's protection must be real."[2]

Is this why we push so forcefully against dormancy, why we try to convince ourselves and others that we can blossom indefinitely without a fallow season? Ceasing to achieve and sitting still in a place of waiting feels deeply vulnerable. The purpose of this discomfort is not misery or despair—though they may be steps along the way. This vulnerability intends to bring "the wholeness, beauty, and adventure of the Kingdom of God to our small sphere of reality today."[3] Can we put aside our self-absorbed kingdoms and lie down in surrender before the mercy of the Creator, waiting for him to make us new? To receive his mind, his Spirit, we must quiet our own and sit, a vessel at rest. For in *him* is abundance, freedom, shalom. In silence, we invite our pain-filled, self-built kingdoms to be conquered and overtaken by wholeness and beauty.

Death, darkness, and dormancy are never the end in themselves—but always, always a preparation for the life and light and abundance to come.

Can we, with God's help, learn to accept and embrace the inevitable, Creator-designed spaces of rest and silence that await us with each breath, each day, each week, and each year? By his design, we cannot live any other way. And, how else will we learn to sit with him and receive that final silence when at last it comes for us?

Walking down the block to unbury the car in sub-zero temperatures, my son remarks dreamily, "I just love winter, don't you? The snow . . . the cold . . ." Then he turns serious and asks, "Are there some places in the country that don't get cold enough to snow? That would be so sad; they can't make snow angels or anything!"

I have so much to learn from my children, the way they

embrace each season for the magic it brings, rarely looking forward or behind, simply receiving the joy and potential in today.

At the first sign of snow, my little (and not-so-little) ones are bundled up and out the door. Within moments, the pristine beauty of pure white has been thoroughly trampled by adorable creatures wearing snow pants. Snowmen and snow forts stand staggered here and there, and a huge rut through the yard shows where they attempted to create a sledding hill on the flat Illinois plains.

Inside the house, I enjoy all this from my warm kitchen, celebrating with Handel's *Messiah* and hot chocolate. From my window, I receive this unrequested gift of rest from a warmer place. But my enjoyment is genuine. After all, watching small children play in the snow is one of the essential joys of life.

Of course, someone gets a snowball in the face, and someone else falls headfirst off the playhouse roof (a safely padded three-foot fall, thanks to the soft snow drifts). Tempers flare and tears fall, and soon everyone has tramped back into the house, peeling off snow-covered outerwear and leaving melting puddles all over the wood floor. Silence is fleeting, after all. Digging deep for the potential of patience (hopefully) cultivated in that one blissful moment of silence, I grab a towel for the floor and start negotiating tempers.

During this dormant season, we are not quite dead yet. Underneath the blankets of sleep and the shrouds of death, new life is being made ready, out of sight.

Thanks be to you, Lord God. We find our rest in you.

CULTIVATING REST

Will you take a moment to sit in silence? Perhaps look out the window or hold a warm drink with both hands—and breathe. Where is there dormancy in your life today? Perhaps life itself seems all but snuffed out, physically or spiritually. Or perhaps life is too much, too loud, too busy, and you crave those moments of recharging that come with each breath, each nightfall, each day of rest.

Can you see God, waiting in these silent spaces, inviting you into them?

- Make time to **turn off the noises**—the TV, the Internet, the phone—and listen to what comes in the silence. What do you hear in the world around you, when you are still?
- **Tune in to the still, small voices**—both your own and the Lord's. What is your body or your spirit telling you, something that perhaps you have been too afraid to hear? What does God's Spirit say to yours when you meet him here?
- **Schedule some rest.** However important and responsible you may be, you will break without times of renewing. Take an hour, or a day, or a week.
- **Allow yourself room to sleep.** Turn off the television or your phone and create a peaceful space to enter when bedtime comes. Receive this as God's gift—and his command. Rest in his presence.

CHAPTER 11

WILDERNESS

Dependence

In the depth of winter, I finally learned that
within me there lay an invincible summer.

ALBERT CAMUS, "SUMMER"

All people are like grass,
and all their faithfulness is like the flowers of the field. . . .
The grass withers and the flowers fall,
but the word of our God endures forever.

ISAIAH 40:6, 8

DRIVING THROUGH the middle of nowhere for ages, my husband and I arrive in the desert, the wilderness. The lush Pacific coast is hours (and a mountain range) behind us. The fertility of the humid Midwest is days (and a greater mountain range) ahead. There are no buildings, signs, or cell towers. Everything, everywhere, is desert.

It strikes me as beautiful, breathtaking. We are vacationing at a state park, not wandering or lost, not desperately fleeing for our lives. We can look at the desolation and see beauty because we have means to escape. To us, this desert is not the ancient enemy, our ultimate impediment to survival. Still, we are very much alone. I can think of no other time in my life I could claim such isolation, so many miles separating me from any human creature. As we climb to the top of a massive hill, wilderness spreads as far as we can see. I snap photos and upload them to Facebook, tagging my location as "Tatooine."

Or I will, later, after we arrive back in civilization. In the desert, even technology—with its ever-present cloud of witnesses—fails to bridge the gap. Without cell service, we can't talk to *anyone*. Vacation or no, the high stakes of the wilderness leave an impression on my psyche. If the car breaks down, if one of us has an accident or emergency, if we thoughtlessly leave our room for the day without water—then what? In the lifeless wastelands, we are utterly dependent.

Where I live, you can't walk to the wilderness. We're surrounded by thousands of miles of towns, cities, suburbs, fields, farms, and forests. Nature, yes, but every bit cultivated, domesticated. Wilderness is a long, long walk away.

And yet, wilderness is a fundamental feature of reality. If we cannot walk into the wasteland, wilderness will come to us. Physically, it comes in drought or cold, no sun to warm the earth, no rain to call forth life. We call it winter, scarcity, famine.

Emotionally and spiritually, wilderness can visit any one of us at any time.

Make or Break

The Bible is stuffed full of wilderness imagery. Because of the geography of Israel, Judah, and Egypt, wilderness was always just around the corner, crouching, lurking, threatening. Like a mortal enemy or epic villain, the wilderness behaves almost as a living character throughout much of the Bible, and the people are constantly formed through encounters with this adversary.[1] Wilderness is the scaffolding and backdrop to their existence,[2] just as the ocean was for my California-grown husband: an immovable reference point.

From earliest recorded history, the ancient world considered wilderness a place of anarchy and danger, spiritually as much as physically. Wilderness was raw material, un-creation, anti-matter, chaos not yet formed into beauty, function, and safety. This is where the evil spirits roamed free, where one met death. It was the opposite of home, of safety, of sanctuary.[3]

And in truth, the wilderness is just such a place. Beautiful and awesome in power, the desert welcomes no one. We cannot wander alone into the wilderness and expect to easily survive. Most of us today live in heavily controlled, risk-averse environments, and the wilderness reminds us just how vulnerable we are, how quickly we weaken and die when exposed to the elements, when removed from shelter, food, and water. Deuteronomy, a book written by a people all too familiar with the reality of the desert, describes it as "vast and dreadful," a "thirsty and waterless land, with its venomous snakes and scorpions."[4] The wilderness is a legitimately terrifying, dangerous place with no guarantee of survival. Here is the force that might defeat even the best and strongest of us, where robbers may attack, where even the most upstanding citizens would fear stopping to help.[5]

Yet in the Bible, the danger and desolation of the wilderness play dual roles. The desert is where men and women are broken . . . or made. It was through wandering the desert that God's people received a new name and identity, an understanding of God, and a purpose. Few servants of God that we meet in Bible stories found their place in his redemptive story without spending time in the wilderness.[6]

Abraham and Sarah, Hagar, Jacob, Moses, Miriam, David, Abigail, Elijah, John the Baptist, Jesus, Paul. Each spent time in the wilderness, whether pursued by enemies, sent by God, or simply journeying forward in faith.[7] An entire nation was formed *into the people of God* when he delivered them from slavery in Egypt and led them straight into the desert. Their forty years of suffering, hunger, thirst, and disorientation are the stuff of legends; following God through a lifetime of wasteland wandering was only marginally preferable to dying as slaves, by their estimation. And yet, in these years of desperate need, they saw water flow from rocks, manna fall from heaven; they gathered under a mountain and saw God come to meet them, forming an eternal covenant between himself and them. With no option for self-reliance, and no buffer between life and death, their dependence on God could be seen, clearly and magnificently.

Could any of this really happen in a land flowing with milk and honey? Do we ever fully throw ourselves upon

God when we have other options? Is there anything that will awaken us to his presence as vividly as utter desperation?

New Testament scholar Gary Burge says,

> The Bible offers no account of a godly man or woman avoiding the wilderness. It is a severe mercy, but a mercy nevertheless. The wilderness experience is where we discover something about ourselves—and God sees what is truly in our hearts. It is here where his simple provisions of water and manna and quail suddenly are seen for their beauty and wonder. And it is here where we might hear his voice in ways unheard before.[8]

For me, vacationing in the desert was a treat, a break from the daily grind, a chance to hike among unique beauty—because I had a hotel room awaiting at the end of the day. But when we find ourselves truly stranded in the wilderness, the high stakes drive us toward God like nothing else. Is it worth the risk? Most of us hesitate, even refuse. We know the truth: We may not survive.

Dark Night of the Soul

Watching the sunrise one glorious morning, I drew my son in close and whispered, "Look, this is what God shows us each morning: The darkness is not forever. The light always comes back." He sat thinking for a moment, then leaned into me, countering, "Yes, but the light does not last either. The darkness always returns too."

Yes, indeed it does. At least, for now.

In spring, we saw hope and despair, how closely they stand together, always in tension, each so very real and present in our lives. Holding to the hope of a sudden spring thaw is worthy and true, but so is the reality of cold, of darkness. Hope persists through the coldest night, but heaviness does too. Deep suffering is real. Despair is vast. Sometimes it wins, overcomes—for a season. As my son knew before he was old enough to tie his shoes, these are the facts of life. No point sugarcoating it.

But God is just as real and present at night as he is at dawn. He made winter just as surely as he created the vibrancy of summer. The facts of life, all of them, are exactly where God can be found. God is in the truth, whatever it may be. In reality, he is in his creation. That is where he has always been.

Why must it be this way? We have been crying out this query since the very first question.

In telling the story of Adam and Eve in the Garden, Walter Brueggemann points out that we rarely ask the most obvious question of all: "Why must there be such dangerous trees?"[9] From the beginning, boundaries are placed on our lives, whether we like it or not. We live, then we die. We have possibilities and expectations. Like my toddlers, we could easily go through life shouting "WHY!?" night and day. Why must this happen to me? Why must I be kept from fulfilling my dream? Why must life be so short and painful? Why must we be so dependent on forces we cannot grasp or comprehend?

So . . . *why must there be such dangerous trees?* And why must there be wilderness, suffering, and despair? Like Adam and Eve and all God's desert wanderers, we are not given an answer either. We can see that these things are true, unassailably present, boundaries to our existence that we did not ask for and cannot understand. We can walk to the very edge of the wilderness, but we cannot move it aside. We cannot fight against these boundaries either, for they will not leave at our request any more than they were created to please us.

A pastor and therapist once wrote that many who came to him for counseling described their lives as "invaded by despair."[10] He named this despair, as spiritually inclined folks have for centuries, a "dark night of the soul." Desolation, sometimes involving long and protracted seasons of suffering, is part of life on earth. There is no formula, no spiritual exercise or magic that will unlock a shortcut, a road that goes only through meadows and sandy beaches and never the wilderness. As the oft-quoted movie *The Princess Bride* points out, "anyone who says differently is selling something."[11]

Thousands of years ago, the exhausted, frightened Hebrews asked, "Can God really spread a table in the wilderness?"[12] Their pain-filled despair and skepticism are memorialized in song: "True, he struck the rock, and water gushed out, streams flowed abundantly, but can he also give us bread? Can he supply meat for his people?"[13]

These old Hebrew stories and songs remain in circulation four thousand years later in part because they resonate so deeply with us—today, and in every era. These men and women *saw* God in the wilderness. As the song goes on to recount, he divided the sea and freed them from Pharaoh with miracle after miracle, besting the magic even of the world's most powerful ruler. He led them boldly into the wilderness with a cloud by day and a pillar of fire by night.[14] Even in the desert, God caused water to flow from dead, lifeless rocks until this most life-giving elixir was as abundant as a river.

Still, they doubted. The psalmist was incredulous—how could they be so dense, so faithless?[15]

Personally, I have no trouble empathizing. They doubted just as I do. My own faith drinks in the sunshine of abundance, then withers with terror and desolation in the wilderness. How do we rest, dependent on our Creator and Sustainer, when everything we know has failed? Can God prepare a table here? *Are you out there somewhere? Can you see me? Do you even remember me?*

The silence of the wilderness can be terrifying. In the wilderness, we are alone but haunted by spirits, by voices, by wild animals and bandits. Just as light is real, so, too, is the darkness. There's no sugarcoating this, no clichés to help us slip past undetected. We may be nearly overcome. But we are not alone, never, ever, ever alone. Our Creator—who formed all the wonder of creation out of desert dust with his own hand, who called out a nation of people to the wilderness and introduced himself to them there by name, who came to dwell among us and wrestled with evil one-on-one in the desert—he has never left.

In the bleakest, deadliest wilderness, he is here.

A Table in the Wilderness

A few years after my husband and I vacationed in the California wilderness, our phones (ever eager to feed us aggregated information to tickle our fancies) sent an unsolicited alert: A rare blooming season was underway in the same desert we had hiked and explored. A combination of unusual weather patterns had converged to create a truly breathtaking explosion of life and color in this barren land—and it would only last a few days.

Of course, thousands of miles—not to mention jobs, plane fare, children, and a million other limitations—stood between us and this epic burst of fertility. Still, we spent an hour poring over pictures online. It was magnificent. Colors we could hardly imagine burst forth, miles upon miles in every shade and hue. It was as though God, in a surge of late-night creativity, grabbed watercolors, turned on some dance music, and got a little carried away. My husband and I marveled, hardly able to envision the barren hills we had trampled through bursting into such flames of pastel.

Yet my incredulity stems only from my ignorance, for this is precisely what the ancients living on the fringes of wilderness knew: Life, if victorious, will burst out gloriously, more vivid and fertile than anything encountered on safer terrain. Deep in the empire of death and desolation, there is a hero's victory to be won.

And so, in airports jammed with travelers heading to the beach, mountains, amusement parks, cafés, and museums, a few brave souls with bulging backpacks embrace the risks, and pilgrimage into the wasteland. The risks are great, the odds stacked so heavily in favor of raw, unbridled cosmos, but those who survive emerge as victors.

The truth I must testify, after journeying over and over, again and again—as certainly as winter follows autumn—is that my times of greatest suffering have been the seasons my Creator plants all the most beautiful seeds. They lie dormant, undetected, for years or decades before any inkling of the beauty and strength that found root in those desert years breaks through the surface. But eventually, they come to light.

Perhaps this explains why the church deeply values fasting, Ash Wednesday, the forty-day journey of Lent, and the dark waiting days of Advent. We grow spiritually fat and lazy when we skip from festival to feast. We won't go into the desert on our own, without being chased, without being called and led and pushed. But there is a prize waiting, if we survive. It is in extreme dependence that the muscles of faith can be tested, stretched, strengthened. We may see God more vividly, he may touch us more personally, than ever before.

In her book *A Beautiful Disaster*, author Marlena Graves writes about the wilderness she wandered during childhood—death, disease, addiction, poverty, harmful decisions, toxic relationships.[16] Yet in the wilderness, God found her, saved her, created her. She says:

> Growing up, I begged God (what seems like thousands of times) to take the cup of suffering from me, but mostly he didn't. Instead, he used my pain and difficulties, my desert

> experiences, to transform me—which in turn alleviated much suffering. As I grew up in the desert, God grew my soul. And although I realize that the suffering I've endured is nothing compared to the suffering of countless millions, I've learned painful but essential lessons that I couldn't have learned anywhere else but in the midst of God-haunted suffering.
>
> God uses the desert of the soul—our suffering and difficulties, our pain, our dark nights (call them what you will)—to form us, to make us beautiful souls. He redeems what we might deem our living hells, if we allow him. The hard truth, then, is this: everyone who follows Jesus is eventually called into the desert.[17]

Graves testifies to the same good news—as incredible as pastel explosions in a wasteland—proclaimed since the beginning of language and the journey of the spirit: the blossoms of the desert are the most breathtaking.

> The wilderness has a way of curing our illusions about ourselves and teaching us to depend more and more on God. When we first enter, we're convinced we've entered the bowels of hell. But on our pilgrimage, we discover that the desert drips with the divine. We discover that desert land is fertile ground for spiritual activity, transformation, and renewal.[18]

It was in the desert that the Creator knelt to plant a lush and fertile garden. It was in the wilderness that the Good Shepherd left behind a flock to find the one who was lost. And it was that same Shepherd who safely led his flock to green pastures and quiet waters.

He will meet you there, too, friend. He will form you and make you and eventually (and maybe not soon) lead you back home.

In the winter, wilderness comes up boldly and settles right at my door. Winds howl with devastating desolation, layers of ice turn the earth into a wasteland. All is dead as far as the eye can see, and should I be stranded without shelter for more than a handful of minutes, my life, too, would succumb to this force of nature, this reality of wilderness. I may live in fertile lands, but I grapple with the waste of wilderness for dark and dreary months each and every year.

When I was young and life felt especially bleak and my heart especially heavy, my dad would sing a little chorus to me: *My Lord knows the way through the wilderness; all I have to do is follow . . . My Lord knows the way through the wilderness; all I have to do is follow.*[19]

I can hear my father's voice, still, when I near the dark night of the soul. The truth of these words coaxes me toward green pastures. Somehow, my Lord *has* always found me: The gentle Shepherd—leaving behind the flock to come and notice me stuck in a ravine, lost in the desert—carrying me back home to green pastures and still waters.

Because he has found me so often in the wilderness, this—more than anything else—is why I am certain he is here at all.

CULTIVATING DEPENDENCE

Friend, have you felt the despair of desolation, of a weariness that seems endless? Rather than pushing this reality aside, sit here for a moment. God is here. He is not scolding you for being lost. He sits with you. However it may feel, *he is already here.* He will lead you through the wilderness.

- Sit or walk quietly, and **pour out your true, honest feelings** to the Lord. Don't try to hold the wolves at bay; simply be honest about this moment. Don't rush past this step. Meet with the Creator *in this place*.
- **Ask for his strength to sustain you,** however long this journey may be. Develop a practice of placing his name on your lips each morning, noon, and night (maybe even set a reminder on your phone).
- **Look for the people or resources he has already given you.** Have friends or family been down this road? Are there lessons you learned years ago which give you hope to hold on to now? Contact these people, and lean on them. Write up the stories, or tell them to yourself.
- When you can, **look for the signs of life** that grow even in despair. Is the sun shining today? Is there a patch of color in a barren landscape? Hold tightly to these things, meditate on them, and remember that he is always, always making things new.

CHAPTER 12

SALT

Endurance

Oft hope is born, when all is forlorn.

J. R. R. TOLKIEN, *THE RETURN OF THE KING*

He has made everything beautiful in its time. He has also set eternity in the human heart; yet no one can fathom what God has done from beginning to end.

THE TEACHER, ECCLESIASTES 3:11

SOMETHING TELLS ME that when Jesus said his followers would be the salt of the earth, he didn't mean the kind of salt that's all over my car. Winter has lingered for months, and it has been very, very cold for a very, very long time. It's discouraging to check the ten-day forecast and see high temps of two degrees below zero (Fahrenheit) as far as the eye can see.

My absolute least favorite part of winter in the northern climates is this layer of salt that accumulates on everything. Creation turns from living, vibrant color to cold, dull gray. Gone is the soft-white purity of diamonds floating down and piling everywhere. Here instead are the relentless remains of toxic, ice-melting residue. My car is not exempt. It doesn't matter if the finish is blue, yellow, or neon pink in the summertime; in winter, the thing is so colorless, it's almost invisible.

If you don't live in these cold, icy regions, you may not have experienced the late-winter doldrums when everything turns gray—but I'm confident you know exactly what I mean. Life feels like this sometimes. As though there's nothing living left, we're just enduring, just waiting for the end. Faith feels like this sometimes. Vibrant and alive during some seasons; dull, chalky, and gray during others. It's tempting to give up, to trade what I have for a more exciting version. It helps me to remember, as I look at my frozen, salty car, that underneath all the dullness and silt the real thing is still there, still beautiful, still good as new.

During these frozen winter months, our job is to get through, to endure.

Spring rains are coming soon.

Darkness before the Dawn

One of the best scenes in literature takes place in Middle-earth, at the foot of Mount Doom in Mordor. Frodo and Sam—two pilgrims on a vital quest—have stayed faithful and true through all forms of temptation, grief, and suffering. They are imminently close to their goal; in fact, they have arrived. Yet "here at the end of all things,"[1] they come also to the very end of their strength. Having endured so much, for so long, worn down by the powerful ring they carry, both hobbits are beyond resilience, desperate yet apathetic to their own despair, unable to see any future at all. They are lost even to themselves.

There is a place beyond exhaustion, beyond discouragement. We have already journeyed through letting go, trusting in the face of loss, accepting dormancy, finding dependence in desolation. How long can we continue putting another foot forward with no evidence of hope? How many times can you come to the end of the rope—only to realize you have no choice but to keep holding on?

These seasons remind me of the transition phase of childbirth. We feel certain that death has arrived, is waiting just outside the door. Yet the irony is that, as anyone who has labored to give birth knows, this moment of complete hopelessness is the signal that life is about to begin, that the season of endurance has nearly come to an end.

Why must this be so? I cannot say. But it *is* darkest just before dawn.

What most of us discover sooner or later is that, at least during some stretch of time, we are given a burden that we have no choice but to carry indefinitely.

When reality covers our spark for life in dull, gray salt, the hardest part can be the haunting questions. Is enduring the best course of action? What does courage look like here? What does contentment mean in this reality? Is this pain and lifelessness a sign to dig deep and keep going, or a wake-up call to dig deep, cut bait, and make a change? How can I figure the way out when I can no longer stand up and look around?

In the end, only Frodo—with the ring burdening his spirit—was unable to lift his body off the ground. Samwise Gamgee found one last sliver of hope, picked up his near-dead friend, and finished the journey—and saved the world.

Lingering at the House of Death

There's a saying in Ecclesiastes that doesn't often find itself embroidered on throw pillows or wall hangings: "It is better to go to a house of mourning than to go to a house of feasting, for death is the destiny of everyone; the living should take this to heart."[2] This isn't likely to be chosen as anyone's life verse, or wind up on the list of passages we're required to take literally as a litmus test of true faith. We *love* feasting! Thanksgiving, Christmas, Sunday dinner, birthday parties, Super Bowl spreads . . . whatever the occasion, bring it on! If offered the choice between a funeral or a feast, most of us wouldn't hesitate. Pass the mashed potatoes.

But the author of Ecclesiastes may be on to something. Feasting is a much-needed part of life, and celebration is an important spiritual discipline. We worship by rejoicing in the fruits of delight and the joys of harvest. But left to our own devices, we would go from feast to feast, from delight to delight, expecting that comfort is the main event. Far too many Christians, discipled in the faith for decades, are shocked to find that faith is not a shield against suffering or death. The regular trials of life feel doubly severe then, for they seem like a bait and switch. Having spent too long feasting, our spirits atrophy, growing unprepared for the reality of death when it comes. The facts of life, instead of pointing us to God's presence, seem to indicate that he has left us entirely—or worse, is untrustworthy, capricious, and cruel.

But it is we who failed to be present. He is right here in the darkest season, more present than the salt covering everything. We have not been exercising the muscles of endurance. Perhaps we ought to take Ecclesiastes to heart after all.

I love to Instagram the lovely flowers of spring, the abundant fruit of my summer garden, the brilliant colors of fall. I even thrill at posting images of the first snow fall, the clean, cold whiteness blanketing the earth. But the dull, dead specters of late winter have never inspired my photography. As far as the eye can see, the earth declares a season of fasting, of mourning, of death.

Today, I considered the dreary stalks of last season's garden standing lifeless among the gray piles of snow and realized I was looking at my own heart. I've worked so hard, endured so long, put my chin down and gone on "adulting," and now hardly any life is left at all.

Feasting in this condition would be a sham, a bald-faced lie aimed at the one who sees my heart laid bare. And so, I sit here in the house of mourning, with my hands held open to the Creator. Without negotiations or false fronts, I plead for the strength to endure, to guard the spark of life I've worked so hard to kindle.

Let us be honest and humble in the face of this mystery, for we are literally at its disposal. We cannot control or command this life or the next. All that matters most is out of our hands, beyond our understanding. The only doorway is trust, trusting the one we have learned through each repetition, the God we followed through pillars of cloud, the face we see so dimly through glass. Linger here, with me, at the house of death, contemplating these hard and complex truths—for truth is where we find him. He is not absent in these lifeless spaces; he is here, and he can be found, even—or especially—in death. Yes, even when dull, gray residue covers everything in lifelessness.

For he exists at both houses, feasting and funeral. In both doorways, his arms are open wide.

This is reality: Existence is beauty and pain in equal and astonishing measure. We must acknowledge that joy and suffering coexist as one and not two, that God has not promised a life free from pain but a life lived *within* pain—and that worship and healing happen only in this place. That God remains with us through the darkest night, present in our most desperate questions. That with this knowledge in our body and soul, we can and will stand, lift our faces and arms, and be fully alive. We must rise and move forward, again and again each day, not in spite of the pain, not with false naive trust, but *with* the pain, and in *perfect* trust.

There is no trick or gimmick, no way to escape. There is only God. And as we endure, as we choose life again and again, we grow stronger. We learn to see him even in the dark.

Friend, this is the truth. This reality is where God lives,

and where we find him, where we worship him. This is the only place where life can be truly and fully embraced. This request, to live abundantly in a world of pain and beauty, is an invitation to *life*.

It is hard, so hard, during the winter seasons of life and of our souls. I tremble with fear at the thought of putting this truth to paper, of saying it aloud, but here is the truth, and with God's help, I summon the courage to say it: *We can rejoice in all circumstances.*[3] With God's help, we *shall* strengthen the muscles of endurance and rejoice, even in the dark. With God as our helper, we will stand in the day of trouble, and we will dance.

We will turn the corner, finally, and discover the first whispers of hope.

About four hundred years ago, the poet John Donne penned a sonnet entitled "Death, Be Not Proud."[4]

> *Death, be not proud, though some have called thee*
> *Mighty and dreadful, for thou are not so;*
> *For those whom thou think'st thou dost overthrow*
> *Die not, poor Death, nor yet canst thou kill me. . . .*
> *One short sleep past, we wake eternally,*
> *And death shall be no more; Death, thou shalt die.*[5]

So, death, we will contemplate you, we will face you, courageously coming forward toe-to-toe, for you are indeed our destiny. But do not let this go to your head. Yours will not be the final word.

Full Circle

I open a late Christmas card and out fall two old photos. One is faded and tattered—a picture of my cousin and me when we were just one-year-olds. The second is more ancient still—a black-and-white image of my grandparents, taken before their marriage the better part of a century ago. They look brilliantly young and beautiful.

I hold both pictures up to show my children, huddled over homework and snacks. My babies are so bright and new, so fresh in the world, so young. With their youth comes all the possibility and energy of a life ahead.

But it also comes with an inability to understand the terms of life that they have no choice but to accept, to receive, to endure. Brand-new to this world, they can have no sense of scope or perspective. My children cannot comprehend their mother as an infant, much less their great-grandparents—now long dead—as young teens heading out into the world.

There are no words I can use to explain to them the certainty of this progression. That these ashes of irretrievable memories were once as real and young as they are now. That my babies, too, will pass through the stages of adulthood to reach where I am and—if they are granted long life—even further.

Likewise, there are no words I know of to teach them the wisdom God gently repeats to us with each gift of breath, every turn of the earth, every trip around the sun. The lesson that weeping remains for the night, but joy comes in the morning. The truth that there is flower, and there is thorn—and God is near to us always and can be found in each one. The knowledge that leisure and delight may give birth to great responsibility, then taper back into quietness. The certainty that the one who set all the stars in motion has never ever left the garden he planted, or the creatures he placed here.

That in staying the course through all these ups and downs, all these turning seasons, we develop the perseverance and understanding to make it through—and the unwavering conviction that we can open our eyes, stretch out our hands, and find him.

Right now. Right here.

I can prepare the way, and tend the soil of their minds and hearts, but I cannot teach them these lessons. These truths are not carried by words but by endurance. The strength to keep walking is learned through experience, through repetition. If they have eyes to see, they will notice the tiny new buds on the trees and the shoots of green that peep through the snow in early spring. They will hold tightly to loved ones in the moment of birth and the hours of death. They will ponder mountains and oceans, kittens and coyotes. They will endure suffering and illness, darkness and pain—but emerge again, and again, on the other side.

I ponder all this, Christmas card still in hand, while they continue shuffling through math worksheets and reading logs. Their homework means the sun is setting on another day. The Christmas card means the earth has completed another revolution around the sun. My grandparents are in the ground and my children are newly born. We keep going around and around and around.

As I head from one year into the next, as so many of them accumulate behind me, the truth becomes ever clearer: We are like the grass, which withers and fades away. But the Word of the Lord endures forever.

Today, my bright blue car and the previously colorful world are entirely covered in salt. There is only gray as far as the eye can see.

But spring rains are coming soon.

CULTIVATING ENDURANCE

Are there areas of your life that seem gray and lifeless, where it seems there is no longer hope for victory? God is here, too, in these places. Even if you cannot see, hear, touch, taste, or feel him—still, he is here. *He is here, he is here, he is here.*

- **Breathe.** This is the main thing we must do to survive each day and the easiest way to worship the God who gives us breath. Draw air in, slowly. Hold it for a second, then breathe it back out—and rest. God is as close as the air we breathe.
- **Use your voice and your body** to reach out to God when your spirit is too weary. Call to him aloud. Sing a song of lament or praise at the top of your lungs. Lift your arms in the air. Walk

through a beautiful place. Touch the beautiful things he has made.

- **Rest. Wait.** This season will not last forever. God's new creation will have the final word. He has been faithful to all generations.[6] The one who began a good work *will see it to completion*.

ENCORE

RESURRECTION

Behold, I am making all things new.

JOHN, REVELATION 21:5, ESV

All shall be well, and all shall be well,
and all manner of things shall be well.

JULIAN OF NORWICH, *SIXTEEN REVELATIONS OF DIVINE LOVE*

ON THE COLDEST, darkest night, when you have nearly given up and cannot believe you will make it until morning, the faintest light appears on the horizon. From the ash piles of the cold, dead flames, one tiny ember is taken by a breath of wind and blown into a spark. Deep within the still, frozen ground lies an unseen seed which begins to look not quite so dead as it once did. The woman crying out in agony after hour upon hour of painful labor heeds her midwife's reminder that when you believe you cannot labor any longer, your body is signaling that your labors are nearly complete.

Since the very first dawning, winter has always, always been made alive by spring. There has never ever been a night so long that it was not awakened by the stirrings of morning. When we look honestly around ourselves, we find that in nature, the seeds of death lie inevitably within life—but just as certainly, life resides buried within the grip of death.

Death, with all its loss and grief, creates the soil, the womb for life to seed, to take root, to thrive and flourish. Each day, my family and I live because something once alive transfers its energy into our own bodies. And someday, our own bodies will break back down into the dust, providing for whatever life comes after us. On this carefully, lovingly fashioned earth, death and life are not two separate beings but are instead two sides of the same coin.

These cycles of life and death, of day and night, are so true, so constant; they repeat themselves again and again, and they speak of the Creator who founded and sustains them.

But there is more.

This Creator came and joined in the dance of birth, life, pain, joy, and death. He came not into mythology but into a country, a culture, a family. He came to us in the same way we come to each other—born as a baby conceived in a woman's womb, formed in her uterus, traveling through her birth canal. Thirty-some years later, the Creator left the same way we all leave—suffering, his body broken, death.

Then, mystery of mysteries, he carried this cycle one step further than we have yet traveled or seen on our own: from life to death to newly resurrected life. Death could not hold the Giver of Life: It burst open, defeated and destroyed. Jesus emerged the victor, the firstfruits of a *new* creation—one that does not follow the pattern we have so carefully committed to memory. This new creation is entirely bewitching, disorienting, and we can hardly imagine it: an inheritance kept safe for us which cannot perish, spoil, or fade.[1] Jesus is the first triumphant herald of eternal spring. He is the promise of shalom, of a world made new.

And so, we insist that death is not the finale: Life will have the final word. Today, sleep always follows waking, just as waking always follows sleep—but one day, we will wake eternally. Death and decay are one stop on the ever-circling wheel, but our Creator does not intend to keep repeating this circle into eternity. Just as he is the Alpha, so is he the Omega. Having set the world in motion, he will bring it to an end, to its telos. To redemption. And like a seed split open in the ground, this end will not be termination, but an eruption of life, of beauty, of *future*.

Resurrection.

Is this the message embedded by the Creator in our ever-repeating world and in our hearts? Might we be placed in this garden primarily to hear the truth our Creator planted on the earth, proclaimed by the sun and stars, that we might learn to hear his voice and meet him in our flesh? The food our bodies need and the food our spirits need—he has placed all of it here, right here. Has he been teaching us resurrection all along? Perhaps all these constant repetitions drive *this one truth* deep into our consciousness: He is always, always making things new.

All that he has placed along my journey on the earth has

spoken loudly of him. I have strained so eagerly to see the outline of his face against the dim and dirty glass. I do not believe that he intends us to wait until this life is over to know him. No, we are meant to learn about him in this life so that when our eyes meet at last, we will not see the gaze of a stranger but the gaze of the one we know fully, even as we also are fully known. He does not ask us to transcend or leave this garden he planted, for we are part of it, and he is here to be found. The Creator will bring creation to fullness, to abundance. Through resurrection, he will bring a groaning creation back to life.

In that dark night of the final winter, after we breathe our final breath, may we open our eyes to the dawning light of new life and find that they are locked on his, seeing face-to-face.

On that morning, it will be spring at last—and all shall be well.

ACKNOWLEDGMENTS

> This my song through endless ages:
> Jesus led me all the way.
>
> FANNY CROSBY, "ALL THE WAY MY SAVIOR LEADS ME"

Where to even begin (or end) my thanks? I can write only because so much has been poured into me, by so many, for so long. I'm tempted to list every family member, friend, and colleague I can remember since childhood—but this space does not allow for that. So specifically, my thanks goes to:

Don Gates, my agent: Thank you for your advice and advocacy, from the beginning to now, and for the last-minute Kentucky barbeque.

Caitlyn Carlson, editor extraordinaire: Thank you for the phone calls, emails, texts, revisions, ideas, and comments. Thank you for reading a thousand versions of the introduction, and for understanding my love of karaoke. You make editing a joy—yes, really.

The rest of the NavPress team: Thank you for the thoughtful way you shepherd your authors, your readers, and Christian dialogue overall. I'm grateful to have fallen in with you. Special thanks to Elizabeth Schroll: You are an incredible investigator of citations. Thank you for your good ideas and hard work. Don Pape: Your passionate investment is such a gift, to me and to so many others. Thank you for being a shepherd. Olivia Eldredge: Thank you for keeping us all on the rails.

The Alliance team at Tyndale: Jeff Rustemeyer, Robin Bermel, David Geeslin, Whitney Harrison, Mariah Franklin! Thank you for all your expertise, professionalism, and friendship. I love working with you all. Eva Winters: I fell in love with the cover at first sight. Thank you for bringing this book to life. And to all the rest of you who proofread, design, stock shelves, and pack boxes: I'm grateful for it all.

Aubrey Sampson: I'm beyond thankful for the miracles that brought your friendship into my life. Thank you for reading everything I send you, for Voxer, and for the spontaneous movie escapes. I'm glad we get to do this together.

All my writing partners, near and far: Afton Rorvik, Sharla Fritz, and Mary Anderson, thank you for your early encouragement and red-penning. This book is stronger because of you. The talented writers at the Redbud Writers Guild, Speaking of Writing, and so many more: You bring the joy of community to the solitary writing life.

Sam Divinagracia, website magician and friend: Thank you for keeping my website working. Without your patience with my frantic texts, no one would ever find me (online). Have fun building your garden.

So many supportive friends and colleagues, too many to count, who opened their emails to find I'd sent a chapter to read *and actually read it and even responded with honest feedback*: Thank you. You have helped me launch books, set up events, gotten excited, or just asked me how I'm doing with it all. I appreciate every single piece.

My parents, Gene and Linda Carlson: Thank you for the babysitting, the dinners, and all you've taught me and poured into me for decades. You've given me everything I have, so, in short: Thank you for everything. My "in-law" parents, Stan and Beverly McNiel: Thank you for all your excitement and support. It means so much to know you've got our backs. Jeff and Melissa Whitmoyer: Thank you for lending me your house in Monterey so I could wrestle with this book in such an inspiring place.

Asher, Benjamin, and Selah: Thank you for being patient with me as I figure out how to live and parent, one day at a time. Thank you for all the fizzy water, special desserts, and *Superstore* episodes when you knew I needed a break. Seeing the world through your eyes is the most joyful gift life has offered me.

Matthew: My longtime partner in life, friendship, and gardening. Thank you for standing so tall and strong in your support of me. All these years that we've held each other up . . . well, that is the biggest thing of all. Your faithfulness and hard work leave me humbled and grateful. Thank you.

And you, dear reader, both friend and stranger: Each time you buy a book, post on social media, write a review, or reach out to me online is a gift I cherish and do not take for granted. I have prayed that you find God in these pages.

And to the Author and Gardener: I create only because I am so enamored by your creation. Thank you for bringing me back to life. My one true hope is that our eyes will meet someday.

May these words of my mouth and this meditation of my heart
be pleasing in your sight,
LORD, my Rock and my Redeemer.

DAVID, PSALM 19:14

DISCUSSION GUIDE

All Shall Be Well is intended to be read and enjoyed either individually or with a group. If you choose to read this book with friends, the questions below may help guide your discussion. Read the listed chapter, going through the questions offered—and then see where the conversation goes! Then, if you'd like, join the conversation online. Post your thoughts on social media using the hashtag #AllShallBeWellBook and see what other readers are saying.

Opening: The Garden

1. Catherine begins by imagining God as a gardener, planting the world by hand as described in Genesis 2. Why does it matter that God is so intimately involved in his creation? Why is it important that God is both transcendent and immanent?
2. What do you think of the idea that God placed repetition in our cycles and seasons to teach us his truth and feed our spirits? What have you learned through observing the cycles and seasons of creation?

Chapter 1. Thawing: *Hope*

1. Describe a time in your life when hope and new life were being kindled, even though everything appeared lifeless and dark.

2. What is shalom and how is it central to the Christian story—from beginning to end?

3. Catherine writes that "death *itself* is not the enemy," that on the earth, where life is sustained through soil and food, death is the womb of new life. What do you think of that? How does this idea point to what God is doing on this earth—and to his ultimate plan?

4. What new life is God cultivating in you today—even in places that look like darkness and death?

5. Did you try the end-of-chapter suggestions for *Cultivating Hope*? What was worth incorporating into your everyday rhythms?

Chapter 2. Clouds: *Faith*

1. Describe a time in your life when you couldn't see where you were going—either literally or figuratively. What did you learn through this experience?

2. Catherine says, "We don't like to hang suspended; we prefer to arrive. But if we can summon the courage to linger and look, mystery may captivate us—and offer

exactly what we need." Do you agree or disagree? Why? What do we need that mystery offers?

3. What are some ways that you have made faith into an idol? How can you let go of your idols? What does God offer in response?

4. What areas of your life or future feel obscured by clouds today? What would help you to lift these areas up to God?

5. Did you try the end-of-chapter suggestions for *Cultivating Faith*? What was worth incorporating into your everyday rhythms?

Chapter 3. Beauty: *Intimacy*

1. Describe a time when you were interrupted by beauty. How did that experience affect you?

2. Do you tend to relate to God more through knowledge/study or experience/relationship? (No wrong answers—both are important!) What does that look like in your day-to-day life?

3. Catherine describes how she sees the truth about her artist friend reflected in her artwork. What does observing God's creation teach us about God?

4. What are some practices that you use to connect intimately with God on a regular basis? How do these practices feed and teach you?

5. Did you try the end-of-chapter suggestions for *Cultivating Intimacy*? What was worth incorporating into your everyday rhythms?

Chapter 4. Heavens: *Wonder*

1. Catherine writes, "Everyone worships *something*. . . . Too often, this something else is my own self." How do the wonders of God's creation affect our worship?
2. Read or skim a few chapters from Job. What is this story—from the devastation to the questioning to the responses—trying to tell us about ourselves and God? How does this sit with you? Does it help? Is it enough?
3. How are awe and worship related to fear and terror? Where does God's everlasting love fit in?
4. How do you prefer to worship? What are some practices you use to engage your mind, heart, and body in the act of worshiping God?
5. Did you try the end-of-chapter suggestions for *Cultivating Wonder*? What was worth incorporating into your everyday rhythms?

Chapter 5. Abundance: *Purpose*

1. This chapter explores a paradox: that God created order out of chaos, then set the ball rolling toward a new kind

of chaos—life and community, with all their messiness. Have you considered this idea before? How does it strike you?

2. What is your personal temperament: Do you prefer calm or chaotic? What does God offer us in each one?
3. *Telos* is defined as "end purpose or goal." What is God's goal for creation, and how does the messy abundance of life help us get there?
4. What do you think is *your* telos, end purpose, or goal? How are you living into that telos in this season? What challenges are you facing?
5. Did you try the end-of-chapter suggestions for *Cultivating Purpose*? What was worth incorporating into your everyday rhythms?

Chapter 6. Toil: *Faithfulness*

1. Describe a time when life was full of labor or responsibility. How did carrying that load affect your overall well-being? What did you learn about God, or how did he feed you, during that season?
2. Catherine claims that the delights and responsibilities of life are intermingled and dependent on each other by design. What do you think of that? How have you seen that interdependence play out in your life?

3. What fruit have you experienced from continuing on the path of faithfulness, even when doing so felt overwhelming? How does commitment to community both lighten and add to the burdens of faithfulness?

4. What practices do you use to stay connected to the source, to receive nourishment, during seasons of pouring out?

5. Did you try the end-of-chapter suggestions for *Cultivating Faithfulness*? What was worth incorporating into your everyday rhythms?

Chapter 7. Harvest: *Gratitude*

1. Describe a time when you experienced the relief of completing something. What did it feel like?

2. What are the traditions and milestones of gratitude that you practice in your communities? Some may be obvious, like Thanksgiving Day. Others might be more hidden, like submitting an annual report or creating a scrapbook.

3. How does celebrating completion and endings affect your outlook on the past, present, and future? What about your perception of identity, whether personal, family, or group?

4. What are you planting and cultivating in your life now? Is this what you hope to harvest later?

5. Did you try the end-of-chapter suggestions for *Cultivating Gratitude*? What was worth incorporating into your everyday rhythms?

Chapter 8. Leaves: *Surrender*

1. Describe a time when you had to let go of something important to you. How did this process affect your identity? Where did God meet you in the surrender?

2. Catherine describes the way trees let go of their leaves in order to live through the winter and create new life in spring. In your experience, how are grief and hope for the future intertwined in the act of release?

3. Jesus taught that in this life, we will find trouble. The Bible is all too explicit in its depiction of trouble, as is our own history. Why do you think we persist in expecting life to be easier than it is?

4. Science suggests that accepting suffering paradoxically limits its power over us, while pushing away negative feelings enhances their strength. What do you make of this? What is your tendency?

5. Did you try the end-of-chapter suggestions for *Cultivating Surrender*? What was worth incorporating into your everyday rhythms?

Chapter 9. Twilight: *Trust*

1. What doorways and thresholds—either literal or figurative—are prominent in your life right now?
2. Read through the passage in John 8 where Jesus calls himself the "light of the world." Why was this a jarring statement? What does it mean for us today?
3. How do we cultivate, over a lifetime, the trust to believe that God is waiting on the other side of every door, no matter how dark?
4. Where do you see Jesus bringing light to the world right now?
5. Did you try the end-of-chapter suggestions for *Cultivating Trust*? What was worth incorporating into your everyday rhythms?

Chapter 10. Snow: *Rest*

1. How do you feel about times of rest? Do you embrace or resist them?
2. What do the natural cycles of dormancy teach us about how God works in the world and how he is working in us?
3. Why do you think we work so hard to avoid silence? What are we afraid of hearing or finding?

4. What practices of rest and silence do you practice? How have they fed you?

5. Did you try the end-of-chapter suggestions for *Cultivating Rest*? What was worth incorporating into your everyday rhythms?

Chapter 11. Wilderness: *Dependence*

1. What role does wilderness or the desert play in the Bible, literature, stories, and in reality? Give examples that you can remember.

2. Have you ever explored a true wilderness? What was that experience like for you?

3. Where have you encountered a wilderness emotionally or spiritually? What was that experience like for you? What did you learn or receive in the process of surviving?

4. Why do you think wilderness times—either physical, emotional, or spiritual—can lead to such deeply rooted growth?

5. Did you try the end-of-chapter suggestions for *Cultivating Dependence*? What was worth incorporating into your everyday rhythms?

Chapter 12. Salt: *Endurance*

1. The saying goes, "It is darkest before the dawn." Do you think this is generally true about life and difficulty? Why or why not?
2. Describe a time when you didn't think you could keep going. What happened then? How did you survive that situation?
3. How do the repetitions and cycles of creation prepare us to survive the hardest, darkest times? How have you experienced these lessons yourself?
4. Throughout the book, Catherine suggests that God's constant, faithful, loving presence has been underlying everything all along. In this chapter, she suggests that when everything is stripped away, we find that "there is only God." What do you think of this perspective?
5. Did you try the end-of-chapter suggestions for *Cultivating Endurance*? What was worth incorporating into your everyday rhythms?

Encore: Resurrection

1. Catherine writes, "Perhaps all these constant repetitions drive *this one truth* deep into our consciousness: He is always, always making things new." What do you see

in the repetitions and cycles that God has placed inside creation?

2. The book ends with a quote that provided the title for the book: *All Shall Be Well*. How does this hope of ultimate shalom fit within the lessons God teaches in these repetitions, and how is it a brand-new thing God introduces?

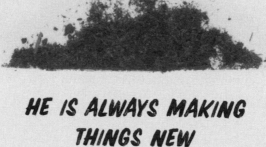

HE IS ALWAYS MAKING THINGS NEW

We all have stories of God doing his creative, redemptive work in the mud and mortar of our everyday moments. Share your stories using the hashtag

#allshallbewellbook

on Instagram, Facebook, and Twitter.

Connect with Catherine as she beautifully intertwines reality with theology. Don't miss her first book, *Long Days of Small Things: Motherhood as a Spiritual Discipline*.

@catherinemcniel

www.catherinemcniel.com

NOTES

OPENING: THE GARDEN

1. A paraphrase of the Creation story in Genesis 2, not to be confused with the Creation story in Genesis 1.
2. Psalm 19:1-4.
3. Margaret Feinberg, *Wonderstruck: Awaken to the Nearness of God* (Brentwood, TN: Worthy, 2012), 51–57.
4. Story from Søren Kirkegaard, as retold in Robert K. Johnston, *God's Wider Presence: Reconsidering General Revelation* (Grand Rapids, MI: Baker, 2014), 1.
5. John 1:9.

SPRING

1. *Collins English Dictionary*, Complete and Unabridged, 12th ed., s.v. "springtime (n.)," accessed January 2, 2019, https://www.thefreedictionary.com/springtime.
2. *Merriam-Webster*, s.v. "spring (v.)," accessed January 2, 2019, https://www.merriam-webster.com/dictionary/spring.

CHAPTER 1. THAWING: HOPE

1. Online Etymology Dictionary, s.v. "Lent (n.)," accessed February 11, 2019, https://www.etymonline.com/word/lent.
2. Bible Hub, s.v. "7965. Shalom," accessed February 11, 2019, https://biblehub.com/hebrew/7965.htm.
3. Cornelius Plantinga, Jr., *Not the Way It's Supposed to Be: A Breviary of Sin* (Grand Rapids, MI: Eerdmans, 1995), 10. Italics in the original.
4. This quote is from Jürgen Moltmann's *Theology of Hope: On the Ground*

and the Implications of a Christian Eschatology (Minneapolis, MN: Fortress, 1993), 16; however, I found it in Mark R. McMinn, *The Science of Virtue: Why Positive Psychology Matters to the Church* (Grand Rapids, MI: Brazos, 2017), chap. 5, "Hope." I am intellectually indebted to both Moltmann and McMinn.

5. Romans 8:24
6. Romans 8:31, 35, 37-39.
7. Romans 8:21.
8. Ecclesiastes 3:20.
9. Psalm 103:15-16.
10. N. T. Wright, "N. T. Wright on Easter, Atonement and the Real Message of the Cross," *Relevant*, April 14, 2017, https://relevantmagazine.com/feature/this-changes-everything/.

CHAPTER 2. CLOUDS: FAITH

1. *Merriam-Webster*, s.v. "theophany," accessed January 28, 2019, https://www.merriam-webster.com/dictionary/theophany.
2. Bible Hub, s.v. "Shekinah," accessed January 28, 2019, https://biblehub.com/topical/s/shekinah.htm.
3. Debbie Blue, *From Stone to Living Word: Letting the Bible Live Again* (Grand Rapids, MI: Brazos, 2008), 15.
4. Blue, *Stone to Living Word*, 21–22.
5. 1 Kings 8:1-13.
6. Hebrews 11:6.
7. William Johnston, ed., *The Cloud of Unknowing and the Book of Privy Counseling* (New York: Doubleday, 2005), 40–41. Emphasis mine.
8. Johnston, *God's Wider Presence*, 40.

CHAPTER 3. BEAUTY: INTIMACY

1. Papa Bear of the Berenstain Bear family employs similar reasoning in searching for a honey tree: "Well, it looks just so. / And it feels just so. / Looks so. Feels so. / So it's SO!"; Stanley and Janice Berenstain, *The Big Honey Hunt* (New York: Random House, 1962), 25.
2. Psalm 63:1.
3. Psalm 84:10.
4. *Seek me and find me*: Jeremiah 29:13; *Come to me and rest*: Matthew 11:28, author's paraphrase.
5. Rich Mullins, "I See You," *The World as Best as I Remember It, Vol. 1* © 1993 Reunion.

6. Jim Manney, *The Prayer That Changes Everything: Discovering the Power of St. Ignatius Loyola's Examen* (Chicago: Loyola, 2011), 3.
7. Michael J. Himes, "Finding God in All Things: A Sacramental Worldview and Its Effects" in *As Leaven in the World: Catholic Perspectives on Faith, Vocation, and the Intellectual Life*, ed. Thomas Landy (Franklin, WI: Sheed & Ward, 2001), 100.
8. You can visit her website at: www.heatherlynnemaynard.com.
9. Romans 1:19-20.
10. Richard Rohr, "Reconnecting to Our Original Identity," Center for Action and Contemplation, February 13, 2018, https://cac.org/reconnecting-original-identity-2018-02-13/. Emphasis in original.
11. Feinberg, *Wonderstruck*, 5.

SUMMER

1. *Merriam-Webster*, s.v. "summer (n.)," accessed January 11, 2019, https://www.merriam-webster.com/dictionary/summer.

CHAPTER 4. HEAVENS: WONDER

1. Niles Elliot Goldstein, *Eight Questions of Faith: Biblical Challenges That Guide and Ground Our Lives* (Lincoln, NE: University of Nebraska, 2015), chap. 2.
2. Job 38:4-11.
3. Job 38:12, 19, 22-23, 28-30, 41; 39:1-2.
4. Job 40:4.
5. Saint Augustine, *The Confessions of St. Augustine*, trans. E. B. Pusey (New York: E. P. Dutton & Co., 1920), 1.

CHAPTER 5. ABUNDANCE: PURPOSE

1. McMinn, *Science of Virtue*, 26–27.
2. NLT.
3. Galatians 5:22-23, NLT.
4. James R. Boyd, *The Westminster Shorter Catechism* (Philadelphia, PA: Presbyterian Board of Education, 1854), 19.
5. John 10:10.

CHAPTER 6. TOIL: FAITHFULNESS

1. Genesis 2:15.
2. *Tend and watch over*: NLT; *cultivate and keep*: WEB.
3. Leslie Leyland Fields, ed., *The Wonder Years: 40 Women over 40 on Aging, Faith, Beauty, and Strength* (Grand Rapids, MI: Kregel, 2018), 10.

4. If you are in an abusive or dangerous situation or relationship, God does not ask you to stay! Please find someone who can help you get to safety, and alert the authorities if necessary. Keeping yourself safe *does not* conflict with faithfulness.
5. From his book title of the same name: Eugene H. Peterson, *A Long Obedience in the Same Direction* (Downers Grove, IL: InterVarsity, 2000). The phrase "a long obedience in the same direction" was originally from Nietzsche. Peterson derived great pleasure from knowing that using this phrase to title a book explaining Christian discipleship would cause the philosopher to roll over in his grave (*A Long Obedience in the Same Direction*, epilogue).
6. Phillip Tovey, ed., *Anglican Baptismal Liturgies* (Norwich: Canterbury, 2017), 109.
7. Matthew 22:36.
8. To read about the Shema, see Timothy Mackie, "What Is the Shema?," The Bible Project, February 18, 2017, https://thebibleproject.com/blog/what-is-the-shema/.
9. Deuteronomy 6:4-5.
10. I first heard this translated "muchness" on "Word Study: Me'od—Strength," The Bible Project, February 15, 2018,: https://www.youtube.com/watch?v=9aaVy1AmFX4. See also BibleHub, s.v. "3966. meod," accessed February 12, 2019, https://biblehub.com/hebrew/3966.htm.
11. Matthew 22:39.
12. Luke 10:29-37.

AUTUMN

1. *Merriam-Webster*, s.v. "autumn (n.)," accessed January 15, 2019, https://www.merriam-webster.com/dictionary/autumn.

CHAPTER 7. HARVEST: GRATITUDE

1. Matthew 5:1-12.
2. Matthew 13:1-9, 31-32.
3. James 5:7, ESV.
4. Galatians 6:8.
5. Paraphrase of a translated Antoine Lavoisier quote found here: https://www.goodreads.com/quotes/143287-dans-la-nature-rien-ne-se-cr-e-rien-ne-se.
6. 1 Thessalonians 5:18.
7. Ecclesiastes 3:1-8; Pete Seeger, "Turn, Turn, Turn (To Everything There Is a Season," *Turn! Turn! Turn!* © 1965 Columbia Records.

CHAPTER 8. LEAVES: SURRENDER

1. Psalm 1:1-3.
2. John 12:24.
3. Bible Study Tools, "Kenosis," accessed February 12, 2019, https://www.biblestudytools.com/dictionary/kenosis/.
4. "God grant me the serenity to accept the things I cannot change, courage to change the things I can and wisdom to know the difference"; typically attributed to Reinhold Niebuhr. To read more about this prayer, see Fred R. Shapiro, "Who Wrote the Serenity Prayer?," *Yale Alumni Magazine*, July/August 2008, http://archives.yalealumnimagazine.com/issues/2008_07/serenity.html.
5. *I can do all things*: Philippians 4:13, NKJV; *Trust in the Lord*: Proverbs 3:5-6, ESV; *For I know*: Jeremiah 29:11.
6. John 16:33.

CHAPTER 9. TWILIGHT: TRUST

1. I first encountered this prayer, whose author is unknown, in David Adam, *The Rhythm of Life: Celtic Daily Prayer* (Croyden, UK: Bookmarque, 2007), 20–21.
2. Sandra McCracken, "Close of the Day," *Gypsy Flat Road* © 2001 Same Old Dress Music.
3. John 8:12.
4. C. G. Jung, *Two Essays on Analytical Psychology*, 2nd ed. (London: Routledge, 1999), 74.
5. C. C. Jung, *The Structure and Dynamics of the Psyche* (Princeton, NJ; Princeton University, 1969), 399–400.

WINTER

1. *Merriam-Webster*, s.v. "winter (n.)," accessed January 17, 2019, https://www.merriam-webster.com/dictionary/winter.

CHAPTER 10. SNOW: REST

1. Genesis 1:5.
2. Jan Johnson, *When the Soul Listens: Finding Rest and Direction in Contemplative Prayer* (Colorado Springs, CO: NavPress, 2017), 31.
3. Johnson, *When the Soul Listens*, 30.

CHAPTER 11. WILDERNESS: DEPENDENCE

1. I am heavily indebted to Gary M. Burge, *The Bible and the Land: Uncover the Ancient Culture, Discover Hidden Meanings* (Grand Rapids, MI:

Zondervan, 2009) for ideas addressed in this section. For the wilderness forming the character of biblical figures, see pages 44–45.

2. Burge, *Bible and the Land*, 38–39.
3. Burge, *Bible and the Land*, 42.
4. Deuteronomy 8:15.
5. The story of the Good Samaritan takes place on the road between Jerusalem and Jericho, which goes through the wilderness (see Luke 10:30-37). Burge's book, cited above, was formative in my thinking here (particularly pages 41 and 44).
6. See Jim Gerrish, "The Wilderness Experience," Word of God Today, accessed February 12, 2019, http://www.wordofgodtoday.com/wilderness-experience/.
7. Burge, *Bible and the Land*, 45–46.
8. Burge, *Bible and the Land*, 47.
9. Paraphrased from Walter Brueggemann, *Genesis: Interpretation: A Bible Commentary for Teaching and Preaching* (Louisville, KY: Westminster John Knox, 2010), 45.
10. Chuck DeGroat, "3 Truths about the 'Dark Night of the Soul,'" *Christianity Today*, February 23, 2015, http://www.christianitytoday.com/pastors/2015/february-online-only/3-truths-of-dark-night-of-soul.html.
11. *The Princess Bride*, directed by Rob Reiner (2015, Culver City, CA: MGM, 1987), DVD. See https://www.youtube.com/watch?v=ThDwS79HPhs.
12. Psalm 78:19.
13. Psalm 78:20.
14. Exodus 13:21-22.
15. Psalm 78:32, 40-43, 56-57.
16. Marlena Graves, *A Beautiful Disaster: Finding Hope in the Midst of Brokenness* (Grand Rapids, MI: Brazos Press, 2014), 5.
17. Graves, *Beautiful Disaster*, 6.
18. Graves, *Beautiful Disaster*, 7.
19. "My Lord Knows the Way through the Wilderness," composed by Sidney Cox. This song was among the repertoire of the Billy Graham International Crusade Choirs: https://www.allmusic.com/album/the-billy-graham-international-crusade-choirs-the-definitive-collection-60th-anniversary-tribute-mw0002183684.

CHAPTER 12. SALT: ENDURANCE

1. J. R. R. Tolkien, *The Return of the King* (London: Harper Collins, 1997), 926.
2. Ecclesiastes 7:2.

3. 1 Thessalonians 5:16-18.
4. Also known as "Holy Sonnet 10."
5. Excerpted from "Death, be not proud," John Donne, public domain; https://www.poets.org/poetsorg/poem/death-be-not-proud-holy-sonnet-10.
6. Psalm 119:90.

ENCORE: RESURRECTION

1. 1 Peter 1:4.